"What a story. Compelling. I am not much of a reader, but this book grabbed me like few others. This book is truly inspiring, with many life lessons for us all. Please read, digest, and then employ the lessons learned. Sixtus's incredible journey, as well as the journey of his father, mother, and family . . . began over a generation ago with his grandparents and parents, and their struggle for survival and a better life in West Africa. It involves the sacrifices of parents to help a son succeed in a world they could not possibly imagine. Sixtus's father had only one request of Sixtus—'give back.' And give back he did."

　　　　—EDWARD C. BENZEL, MD, emeritus chairman of
　　　　Neurosurgery, Cleveland Clinic

"As the world becomes smaller, stories like Sixtus's remind us of the awesome opportunities and responsibilities that come with the ever-shrinking world. Read this and be moved. You will be a better person ready to do great things for God."

　　　　—MARK LANIER, lawyer and author of *Christianity on Trial* and
　　　　Psalms for Living

"A story that brought joy to my heart! An adventure that continues. An inspiration."

　　　　—CLARKE E. COCHRAN, PHD, professor emeritus of Political
　　　　Science, Texas Tech University; author of *Religion in Public and
　　　　Private Life*

"This is an amazing story by an amazing man. His father gave him many gifts, especially that of a servant's heart and acknowledgment of the Divine intervention that led him to accomplish so many things at this point in his life. Sixtus is a man of great character and a devout Christian. This story is not yet complete. I look forward to seeing what he will accomplish in the coming decades."

—DR. DUNCAN BURKHOLDER, MD, chief medical officer, Grace Health System

"Meeting Sixtus in person is a testament to recognizing the definition of 'force of will.' Reading his personal and family history allows all of us the opportunity to recognize the origins of that force—the sacrifice and faith that have allowed him to become an inspiration to so many in West Texas and around the world. In a time of division, his human warmth and accomplishments on page after page are beyond inspiring! Read this, feel how it stirs your soul, and challenge yourself to help others in this way!"

—BRYAN MUDD, news anchor, KAMC-TV, Lubbock, Texas

"After experiencing a mission trip firsthand with Sixtus, this book perfectly portrays his journey and his mission! There's nothing more fulfilling and encouraging than learning about the obstacles that Sixtus overcame to achieve not only his dreams, but his father's dreams! This is one of the most inspiring and fulfilling books, offering an abundance of wisdom and inspiration!"

—HANA QUBTI, Purpose Medical Mission volunteer

"An incredible heart-wrenching and heart-warming story. A lesson in integrity, tenacity, hope, faith, charity and love. And a powerful reminder that God is the Father who is guiding all of our lives."

—DR. EMILY DEEB, MD, Purpose Medical Mission volunteer

"*My Father's Gift* is the story of the profound impact of a father's sacrificial love on his son's life and the lives of many others. Starting with the privations of a primitive life in Cameroon, Africa, and ending with a quintessentially American success story, Sixtus relates a terrible, wonderful tale. His success, given his beginnings, seems unlikely, but underneath all is a tremendous drive, born of equal parts desperation and gratitude. This is a real-life story you will not want to miss. A testament of the human spirit, and of God's ever-present, directing hand in the life of a young boy, which later has significant reverberations for the health and well-being of countless lives across continents."

> —**KATHERINE LINCOLN**, associate professor,
> Tarleton State University

"*My Father's Gift* depicts a vivid illustration of a humble beginning of a young man from a noble background to pursue his very best in personal identity through an incredible and uplifting journey that cumulates in love and service in his career and lifestyle. Sixtus's intricate story will uplift and edify any reader with a rewarding experience. A brilliant and fantastic piece of work for all to read and discover how the affluence of family can be a life changer for self and others."

> —**MARGARET K. MBESEHA, PHD**, special education
> consultant, Nwankem Benevolent Foundation Inc.

"This is an important book and deserves to be read and shared and gifted. Mr. Atabong, and his father through him, tells the story of how the blessing of the Father is the seed that bears much fruit. Out of the most unlikely place, a village in Cameroon, Atabong's story becomes our story, and his passion for the human family has taken root in the most unlikely of places, West Texas."

> —**TOM STANTON**, general counsel and vice president of the Texas
> Methodist Foundation; director of Congo Projects for Relief; volunteer
> in mission to DR Congo for thirteen years.

"*My Father's Gift* is a story of faith and passion. Moving. Sixtus's story inspires all to serve."

> —**DAN POPE**, mayor of Lubbock, Texas

"Sixtus has been able to apply the leadership skills that were instilled in him by parents, teachers and mentors to give back to his community in Cameroon, Lubbock, and the needy in Central America. This book is an inspiration to all immigrants in the diaspora."

> —**EKOKOBE FONKEM, DO**, associate professor of Neurosurgery,
> Baylor Scott & White HealthCare and Texas A&M University, CEO of
> Healing Beyond Our Horizon.

"This book clearly defines what it means to be a leader in your profession. It's not about a title, or status, or money, or power. It's about serving others, having a vision, never giving up, being confident and humble at the same time, and having the courage and determination to a make positive difference in your community. Every PA, PA student and pre-PA should read this book. "

—LINDA C. DELANEY, MPAS, PAC, past president of the Texas Academy of Physician Assistants, past director at large of the American Academy of Physician Assistants

"This is a beautiful story about a family being each other's keeper and acting on the father's request that they give back to others."

—OBIE L. STALCUP, MD, chief of Urology, Grace Clinic

"From Cameroon to Lubbock, Sixtus Atabong 'dreamed no little dreams' and made them come true through hard work and perseverance. Now, through his work as a physician assistant and as the founder of Purpose Medical Mission, Atabong is paying it forward in West Texas and across the world. What an amazing life."

—KENT HANCE, former chancellor of the Texas Tech University System, former US representative for Texas's 19th District

"Sixtus is a man of purpose and conviction who loves God and has a passion for serving others. He is a dear friend and someone who inspires me to be more and do more to make the world a better place."

—US CONGRESSMAN JODEY ARRINGTON, Texas's 19th District

"Sixtus's story is an engaging, intimate, inspiring and very personal account of one man's challenges coupled with his sheer determination to give back to his community in return for the sacrifices made by his tenacious father, which afforded him the opportunity to become a healthcare provider. Sixtus defines what it means to be a true servant leader, and he pays homage to the foundation of the physician assistant oath by serving and caring for others."

—JAMES E. DELANEY, PA-C, past president of the American Academy of PAs, past president of the California Academy of PAs

My Father's Gift:
How One Man's Purpose Became
A Journey of Hope and Healing

by Sixtus Z. Atabong, PA-C

© Copyright 2018 Sixtus Z. Atabong, PA-C

ISBN 978-1-63393-675-1

Published by

 köehlerbooks™

210 60th Street
Virginia Beach, VA 23451
800–435–4811
www.koehlerbooks.com

MY FATHER'S GIFT

HOW ONE MAN'S PURPOSE BECAME A JOURNEY OF HOPE AND HEALING

SIXTUS Z. ATABONG, PA-C

VIRGINIA BEACH
CAPE CHARLES

TABLE OF CONTENTS

DEDICATION

To my wife, Kyu Mee, for believing in me when it seemed I was going nowhere but downward. Now that I have everything any man could ever hope for, you have stayed the same person—humble, caring and loving. You helped reinforce my belief that every human interaction is an opportunity to assist each other, and to find our purpose in life. I am inspired by your spirit. You will always be the love of my life.

Aspire to Inspire before you Expire.

FOREWORD

IT IS MY GREAT honor to be asked to write the foreword for Sixtus Atabong. His story is a remarkable one of humility, courage and triumph. Even though the book on the surface would appear to be a salute to his father, it is in fact to his whole family and the people of Cameroon.

I first met Sixtus about three years ago when I was invited to speak at a fundraiser for "Purpose Medical Mission" in Lubbock, Texas. I was introduced by a mutual friend, Dr. James Burke, who was one of my teachers and mentor when I attended Texas Tech University School of Medicine. He called and said, I want to meet a young man who is driven to give back to his community. This was followed up with a phone call with Sixtus, where I realized that I had to support him any way I could. So, I agreed to speak at the event. During the program, as he explained to the audience about the mission of the organization, I was thoroughly impressed. Here was a guy who truly cares and is committed to ensuring that others had adequate medical care, particularly in the poorest countries.

As you read his book, you will discover the reason why Sixtus is so passionate about this mission. It started with a simple gift from his Father at an early age. Not to give the story away, let's just say that it was "a gift for a lifetime." It began in his early childhood and his relationship with his family, particularly with his father, who was the primary caretaker. In his father's explanation of the relationship with GOD, when young Sixtus asked, he said that we are made in God's image and that our role is to "Strive to do our part." This set the course for this eight-year-old child's love with Christianity and the stage for a purposeful, driven life.

Another gift from his father came during his early education, when his sacrifice would enable him to go to prominent school even though, by many standards, he could not afford to attend. Sixtus was always appreciative for this opportunity, because without it he would not have been educated or in the position to come to America. But greatest lesson learned was "humility" from selfless acts of his father. You need to read further to discover how.

It was during his first year in America that Sixtus fell in love with his adopted country, but always keeping Cameroon in his heart and mind. And it was Texas where he found his ultimate vocation and the love of his life. This book is a love story of a sort. An African son finding himself and his life in the high plains of Texas.

Pursuing his medical training as a Physician Assistant (PA) gave him the ability to help those in need, especially his family and friends back home. In this book, you will learn that Sixtus has an unlimited capacity for charity, despite many trials and tribulations, despite how he was treated by his own countrymen. The old adage, "What doesn't break you makes you stronger." Stronger indeed. I believe that it was those lean years, those painful years, that laid the foundation for this man today. He was fortunate to become part of a loving community of Lubbock, Texas, and to have completed his training at Texas Tech University Health Sciences.

Sixtus said, "I realized that my entire life had been built upon one gift after another—some from people I knew and some from others that I did not know. Some I would have the opportunity to repay; others I would never meet again, at least not in this lifetime," and "Our purpose on earth is to serve others as others have served us."

These quotes are the linchpin of the creation of a Big Plan and Journey to Purpose, that would eventually lead to Purpose Medical Mission. The organization that he founded over ten years ago, brings hope to despair. One of the challenges that he makes in the book is . . . how collectively we can use charity to foster human dignity. For him, it's about providing hope to the hopeless and empowering individuals and communities to fulfill their dreams. A sentiment that we share.

In chasing the American dream, he met his wife, Kyu Mee, who became his accomplice in providing purposeful medicine and purposeful charity not only in Cameroon, but throughout the world. These two are a force to reckon with. An unstoppable force for good, in a world filled with much despair. Purpose Medical Mission was formed to be a bridge of medical assistance to severely medically underserved communities around the world.

I would be remiss if I did not mention the role that his Mother has played in his upbringing, and in the establishment of his values and willingness to open his heart to people. There is an old African-American saying: "If a child is born with their hands closed...they will be stingy, but if their hands are open...they will be free-hearted." Meaning that they will be caretakers with open hearts, giving freely to those in need. From the description of his Mother, I am sure that he received this gift from her.

Sixtus not only serves as a role model for all of us in giving back, he is paying it forward through the parenting of their two boys. His story is one of Family Legacy.

It has been a pleasure to get to know him . . . and his work. As you read this book, you will now get an opportunity to know him too. I believe that you will come away with same conclusion that I did . . . a son of Africa, who is also a shining star of the American Dream.

—Bernard A. Harris, Jr., MD

Astronaut
Author of DREAM WALKER: A Journey of
Achievement and Inspiration

INTRODUCTION

I WAS INVITED BY a friend for an early Saturday morning coffee at Starbucks to meet with a gentleman from Austin, Texas who had done extensive mission work in East Africa. He is a successful businessman who was born in Snyder, a small town in West Texas. He was visiting his family to celebrate his grandfather's 90th birthday. They had helped build a church and provide solar energy to several communities in South Sudan. While in South Sudan, he was touched by the complete lack of healthcare in the region and was praying for guidance on how he could help. Not being in the medical field, he faced many challenges. His goal was to help the people build a sustainable medical clinic. He wanted to seek my advice.

We spent two hours talking about each other's work and the fulfillment that comes with saying "yes" to a call to serve. I was seeing him off to his car, and he asked me, his full cup of coffee still in his hand, how I ended up in West Texas. We both had a very busy day ahead, so I gave him a brief version of my own story. He then asked me if I had ever considered writing a book about my life. I thanked him and told him that I didn't write, but he persisted. If not a book, he said, I needed to keep a journal or write a memoir for my kids, as no one would be able to tell my story better. The last thing he said to me before getting in his car was, "Sixtus, you should aspire to inspire before you expire."

Well, David, thank you. Here we go . . .

CHAPTER 1

THE CARETAKER

AS A CHILD, I never understood why Dad proudly accepted the villagers' nickname *Idi Amin Dada*. It was a nickname he acquired after the infamous president of Uganda from 1971 to 1979, who was portrayed in the 2007 movie, *The Last King of Scotland,* as the eccentric brutal Ugandan dictator. To the young men in my village, the name might have been well deserved. For me, he was just Pa John Atabong—my father, my inspiration, my hero.

Pa John was born in Bellah Ngeh, into a polygamous family with three wives, during a period of extreme poverty and an infant mortality rate of over 90 percent. He came into this world in his parents' house, made of red mud, roofed with thatches, and located on one of the many steep hills of what is now commonly called Fontem, in the South West Region of Cameroon, West Africa. He was the last of his mother's twelve children, only three of whom would survive into adulthood. Nine of his siblings had died at birth or during their first few years of life, leaving my father and two older brothers. There is no document of his date of birth, so any reference to his age would be an estimate based on a timeline of stories gathered from him and family members.

His parents had a small farm where they raised crops,

mostly for home consumption. Though my grandparents had no formal education, they wanted to send their children to school. They couldn't afford to send all three boys to school, and they still needed help on the farm. They decided to pick the most intelligent of the boys to send to primary school. After months of secretly observing the boys, they picked the second oldest son. My dad was devastated, but at the age of ten there was nothing he felt he could do about that decision. He still wanted to go to school like a few of his friends in the village.

Just a year after his brother started primary school, their father died, leaving behind his mother to care for them. Without a husband, she neither could afford her son's education or food for her family. She desperately needed to find a way to support her three young boys, so she met with a local witch doctor who was also a traditional healer and a fortune teller. The healer advised my grandmother to take her three sons out of the village to escape a jealous witch who was killing off rivals through witchcraft. During this time, the Bangwa people of Fontem mostly practiced traditional medicine with traditional healers as their doctors, and local chiefs were rulers. Witchcraft was widely accepted and practiced. This was a time when women were seen and considered as second-class citizens who couldn't own property and were not allowed to work outside the home. World War II was still being fought, and the fear was that developed nations were recruiting fighters from their foreign colonies. If my grandmother took her sons to the coast, they could be forced to fight in a foreign war or work in plantations with little or no compensation.

By the age of eleven, my father had become quite skilled at harvesting palm oil and selling the produce at the local village markets. The work was quite labor intensive, but he needed to support his family and help pay for his brother's education. His work involved climbing thirty-plus-feet-tall palm trees to harvest the palm nuts. Then he would spend days, with the help of his mother, producing the palm oil. Compared to the other villagers, he had become quite successful. But my grandmother, afraid he might get harmed by the local "witches" out of jealousy, sent her son to live with a family friend in a distant village called

Letia. My father's newly adopted father was nicknamed Pa Moni.

My father continued to produce oil, but this time he had to split the little profit he had with the owners of the palm trees and the land. The work became quite tedious for him and there was very little return to support his family. So he had to find another way. He had heard of merchants who traded goods in a distant plantation town of Meanja, approximately 200 miles from his village. He wanted to go there and see if he could find work. With his mother's blessing, he accompanied the merchants on a one-week trek through jungles, climbing hills, and crossing rivers and mountains from Fontem to the coastal town of Meanja in Muyuka subdivision. He did this barefooted because he did not have enough money to own shoes, typically made out of rubber for long walks. They would only stop to rest in strangers' homes, some of whom provided them food and others who just offered space for them to rest. My father was approximately thirteen at the time. Most residents in this new village of Meanja were plantation workers who owned little or no private property themselves.

The Germans had ruled Cameroon until the end of World War I when they lost control of the colony to France and Britain. During their rule, the Germans had developed vast plantations of rubber, banana, tea and palm using forced labor, especially in the coastal areas. After World War II, Southern Cameroon was made a United Nations Trust Territory under the colonial rule of Britain as a mandate territory.

When World War II was over, news traveled into the villages: there were opportunities in the coastal regions. Laborers were leaving plantations and using their skills to develop private farmlands. Villagers were told that they could own land with little money, and that they could help the "white man" build roads, even without a formal education. They could also be plantation truck drivers without a driver's license. These stories mostly came from laborers and loggers who were hired to transport timber from the forests to the seaport in the major port city of Douala for export to Europe.

Father immediately applied for a job as a worker but was told that he needed to learn English, French or pidgin English (Creole), a language that emerged in this part of Africa from the interaction of the local population and the British during the time of slave trading. However, he was given a shovel and one of the lowest jobs in the plantation—to work the roads and shovel gravel into the potholes. It didn't take him much time to learn Pidgin English and make friends with the plantation and timber drivers.

One of these drivers was Mr. Ferdinand. After hearing many of his stories, my father approached him to become his "boy boy" apprentice. He would do all the hard labor free of charge and in return, Mr. Ferdinand would teach him how to drive. After about eighteen months into training, and with Mr. Ferdinand's recommendation, my father passed his driver's test. He still couldn't get the highly sought out jobs at the plantation because he was illiterate. He applied to several places but was eventually hired by the Muyuka Rural Council as a dump truck driver.

After five years of working with the council with little and sometimes no pay, my father began planning his next move. The workers were aware that money allotted for them was often embezzled with impunity by the government officials who were supervising them. Unfortunately, whistle-blower protection was nonexistent, so no one dared to complain about these bad practices.

As a truck driver, my father drove through several small remote villages and frequently stopped to take breaks. One of his favorite villages was Munyenge, about sixteen miles from Muyuka. He noticed that the land was very fertile, but few people farmed the land. If he could just own a parcel, he thought he could grow crops to sell to other truck drivers and residents in surrounding towns. Since the chiefs were the landowners in that part of the country, my father would need to forge a relationship with one of them, and then convince him to sell a piece of land. But first, he needed to check on the status of his future wife. He sent a message to his mother in Bellah and his adopted father, Pa Moni in Letia, to go visit my mother's parents.

According to the culture, your family could pick your wife for you at a very early age. In fact, the earlier the better. So at just twelve years old, my father knew who his wife would be. Because the chiefs and the more successful villagers could marry unlimited wives, there were fewer women for the other men in the village. In addition, you were expected to marry only from your tribe.

Pa Moni was a very good friend and neighbor to my mother's dad. My maternal grandmother was pregnant with her fifth child. Her first three girls had all survived and had already been promised to three local chiefs. When my father moved in with Pa Moni, his uncle was very impressed by his hard-working nephew. He wanted to help the boy secure a wife. So, Pa Moni kept a close eye on the pregnancies of my maternal grandmother. He knew the family well. All the girls were well-behaved. Certainly, if the next baby was a girl, she too would be beautiful and most likely grow up to be a great wife and mother.

On the day of my mother's birth, Pa Moni heard that my grandmother had delivered a baby girl. He sent for my father's mother and both of them paid a visit to my mother's parents. They took with them five pieces of firewood, which were burned in my mother's compound, signifying the newly born baby girl would become my father's wife if she survived to the age of 18. My mother's parents accepted, they exchanged gifts, and the rest is history.

Now that my father was beginning to see a glimpse of hope in his future, he needed to make sure that the wife he had been promised was still available. He had a plan mapped out in his head that included my mother, who at the time was only about age ten. Because the village chiefs were very powerful, my father worried that one of them would take his future wife for himself, and my mother's parents would have no say in the matter.

My father wanted his future wife to learn Pidgin English and a trade. But my mother's parents couldn't afford to send her to school. Between my mother's parents, my father's mother and Pa Moni, they decided to send my mother to live with Ma Esther, one of my father's aunts. My father would send money for her to learn embroidery and sewing. So she lived with my father's aunt for six years, and then went back to her home in Fontem for the final preparations before she would join my father. After two additional years of fulfilling traditional requirements and approval from the elders and chiefs, my father was finally allowed to take his wife to their home in Muyuka. She was about eighteen years old.

One afternoon on his way to work, my father stopped in Munyenge to visit the village chief. He had brought wine, rice, whiskey and other gifts. After a long visit, he proposed to the chief that he wanted to buy some land and eventually intended to move to the village to farm. The chief agreed, and a price was set. My father now had his wife and owned several pieces of untouched land. He started clearing the forest, initially by himself, and making room for crops such as cocoa, coffee, yams and potatoes. He and my mother sold their crops at the local markets and used the money to buy more land. They built their first home in Munyenge using wood from their farms. Dad went back to Fontem and brought his mother and two brothers to live and work with him. He would eventually convince most of his friends and other family members, including Mr. Ferdinand, to leave their plantation jobs and join him in his newly found home of Munyenge village.

With the additional help, my father soon was producing more crops and now needed access to the bigger, more profitable markets in other towns and cities. He reached out to a friend in Douala to help him buy his first farm truck. He was the first-ever truck owner in the village. Before bringing the car to the village for the big celebration, he stopped at a paint shop in the city of Douala to have the name he had carefully picked out boldly painted on the sides of the truck: *Operation Feed The Nation*. He believed he alone could solve the problem of hunger in the entire country of Cameroon using the food crops that his farms were now producing.

Driving to and from the market allowed him little time to focus on full-time farming, so he decided to recruit villagers to help him farm. He would teach them how to farm and then offer them the gift of a piece of his farmland. They would be expected to split the profits from cash crops with my father. It was sort of a trade-by-barter arrangement. They were encouraged to plant any other crops they wanted for their household consumption. Within a few years, he and the farmers were making enough money to take good care of their families.

My father became the most successful farmer in that region and was named *Fua-keh'bin* (king of the forest) by his fellow farmers. He and my mother had five daughters in about nine years. Dad and Mom took care of many other children, as they believed the gods had blessed them and so they should share those blessings with others who were less privileged. The one thing they felt was missing was a son of their own.

Banana plantation.

My ancestral village of Fontem.

My childhood home in Munyenge village, and my parents' first home.
Two small buildings in the front were for storage of farm goods.

My mother. This picture was taken in a studio in Muyuka
during her early years of marriage when she was about 20.

My parents during their first year of marriage.

Palm nuts harvested from palm trees.

Palm oil used for cooking.

Palm trees. My father climbed these trees to harvest palm nuts
that were processed to produce palm oil.

The house my father built for his brothers after moving them from Fontem to Munyenge.

CHAPTER 2

THE BIRTH OF A SON

IN THOSE DAYS, IT was not unusual for a family to have more than five children. The reasons were three-fold. First, families never knew which child would survive to adulthood. Secondly, more children also meant more farm hands, increased productivity and profit for the whole family. Lastly, as parents grew old, the role of caretaker went to the children. More children meant that role could be distributed among many instead of a few. However, the popular expectation at that time was that girls would marry into a different family, so only the boys would inherit and foster their family name and legacy. Even with all his success, Dad still felt all his hard work would be in vain if he did not have a son to carry on his legacy. The superstition in rural villages was that a prosperous farmer without a son must have made a deal with the dark powers—his sons in exchange for wealth. My father did not want that taint.

Though Dad knew there was a God, he didn't know much about Christianity. He had been introduced to the faith by Catholic and Protestant evangelists, but always brushed them off and would advise them to get a real farm job and stop extorting people. He had been to the Catholic Church several times, usually during celebrations, but he still had doubts about the existence of the one God. He admitted that sometimes he would contemplate the beauty of his surroundings, and its relation to his existence. The one thing he was certain of was that hard work led to success.

It was a cloudy day in July 1974 when he had his first communion with God. It was the season for insect control. At the break of dawn, he made it out to his cocoa farm with his insecticide supplies. The crew worked for hours on end and stopped for a break only if it rained, because the rain would wash away the chemicals immediately. They strapped on their back a ten-gallon tank of water mixed with insecticides, with the pump on the left hand and sprayer on the right. Rainwater in barrels throughout the farm was used to remix and refill whenever the workers ran out of chemicals. They would repeat the drill several times throughout the day for up to three months, and would only stop for harvesting season.

On this fateful day, the rain poured. Dad couldn't make it back to the farmhouse, so he found shelter beneath a tree. He took a short nap and dreamed that Mom was pregnant with a boy. He awoke and envisioned life with a son he could go to the farm with. He thought, *If this God does exist, he should know my heart's desires and give me a son.* He went down on his knees, raised his arms up to the sky and made a deal with God—*since I have no enemies and I've taken care of many, and I've worked hard all my life, you should bless me with a son.* He went home and told my mother of his promise to God, asking her to help him keep this covenant should they be blessed with a son.

Good news came three months later. Mom was carrying another baby. But would this be the long-awaited boy my father had asked for? There were no ultrasounds or laboratory tests to tell, so everyone had to wait nine months to find out.

With the rumors in town that father was not capable of having a son, he decided to make a very friendly bet with the village chief, who at this time was his very good friend. Because all of father's farms were far from the house, he had always wanted a farm closer for my mother and the girls to plant non-cash crops for home consumption. However, the properties around the village were forbidden land, reserved for the chief and his family. So the chief entered a verbal agreement with my father: if my mother gave birth to a male child, he would give my father a piece of farmland close to the village. In return, Dad would name his son after the chief.

With every passing day for six months, Dad performed nightly prayers with the family. He bought a four-pound King James Bible and asked his children and strangers to read it to him. He wasn't afraid to show his newfound friendship with God by buying the biggest Bible he could find.

In those days, most women delivered children at home, and only those who could afford it travelled to the closest government hospital. Since it was impossible for a pregnant woman to know her delivery date, she and a family member would travel to the hospital vicinity and find a home to live in near a hospital. This period of uncertainty sometimes lasted for weeks or even months, especially for first pregnancies.

Dad had decided that this child, like the previous five, would be delivered at Mount Mary Hospital in Buea, the provincial capital of this region in Cameroon. This was a Catholic mission hospital about thirty miles away. It served wealthier government officials and was run by European missionary physicians. Mom went ahead and Dad planned to follow to Buea three weeks before delivery. They stayed with a distant relative a few blocks from the hospital.

On the day of delivery, my father sat outside the delivery room and waited. After delivery, a nurse came out to notify him of the birth. He gave thanks to God. Mom asked her if she had told him the sex of the child, and the nurse responded that she hadn't. *"My pikin, e get five girl pikin dem and e don di wait for boy pikin. Abeg go tell yi say na boy pikin,"* Mother explained to her that her husband has five girls and is very anxious to find out the sex. She asked the nurse to go back outside and tell him that it's a boy. The nurse went back outside and asked my dad why he didn't inquire about the sex of the baby. Dad responded that he was too anxious to find out. The nurse then announced to him that he was the father of a baby boy.

Dad took off in a state of elation. He gathered some friends and passersby in Buea and a nearby town of Muyuka to celebrate with him. It would take him about twenty-four hours, and on April 1st he made it back to Munyenge. He proudly announced my birth, the birth of his first son, as he entered the village. They all thought it must have been an April Fool's Day joke. As it was customary during this time, because of the high infant mortality rate, newborns were kept in the hospital for weeks, even months. My dad was asked by one of his brothers how the baby was doing, and he replied that he was so overjoyed and eager to share the news that he forgot to see the baby. It was also not unusual for men to go days before seeing their wives and new babies. It would be another three days before a delegation from the village accompanied father to come for me.

Mom and Dad went on to have three more girls and another boy. They were also blessed with numerous adopted children. Their faith in God would grow with children, and Dad's dedication to impact his surrounding would also grow. Together they worked hard to keep his covenant with God. Dad made sure we all had a role in the local church. The girls were mostly involved in choir and cleaning the church, and I, the only son for a while, was responsible for waking up every morning to go ring the church bell for morning prayers. Initially, Dad would accompany me in the early morning darkness to show me how to ring the bell, which was a tire wheel drum mounted on a tree in front of the church. This was loud enough to be heard across our small village. Dad would also get me involved as a Mass server and altar boy. After morning prayers, Dad would go to the farm while Mother would stay behind to prepare our lunches, then meet up with Dad at the farm while the children would head off to school. After school, we would join them and help carry the crops back home. This became our daily routine for years.

Even with his commitments and assistance to the church, my parents were not allowed to take communion, as they were neither baptized nor married in church. In 1984, they enrolled in a Bible study program and a pre-marital baptism class. Each of the kids would take turns going with them to class because they could not read or write. We would take notes and review the lessons nightly as a family. Mom and Dad would eventually get baptized and have their official church wedding in 1985, more than twenty years after their traditional marriage.

Growing up as the only son, I always looked forward to the summer holidays when I would accompany my dad to the farm. Most of the time, it was just the two of us. After the cocoa harvest, we would go back to the farm to dry the cocoa beans. This process took about two months and we often stayed at the farm for days without going home. These were my most cherished moments with my father. During the day, he would tell me his life stories. He would ask me to read the Bible to him and he would give me his interpretation of every verse. I would listen to him attentively and wonder how someone with no education could have so much wisdom and understanding of the Bible and our role on this earth. With him, I read the entire Bible several times. When he had a lesson to teach, he would ask me to find a particular chapter and verse. Occasionally, I would fall asleep during his explanations and he would wake me up in frustration, much like Jesus woke his disciples several times at the Garden of Gethsemane.

Dad explained how wonderful it was that God, who has everything and was capable of doing anything, would want to create me in his image. He asked me to reflect and consider what that meant and how it made me feel. He emphasized that everyone was created in God's image. He said to me, "If I look like God and my neighbor looks like God, then who exactly does God look like?" While my eight-year-old brain was still pondering, he told me how God must look like all of us. He explained that the most important lesson is that we are all created in the image of God, something we should be very proud of. To Dad, this was the foundation of human dignity. It is our identity and we should embrace it, defend it and foster it.

Dad went on to explain to me in his very simple terms how we make up the body of Christ regardless of our occupation or financial status, and that all people have a vital role to play. As each part of the human body relies on the others, so must we all, who make up the body of Christ, strive to do our part. He explained that it is our duty to first figure out our function, and then help each other to find theirs. And no matter how big or small our role might seem, God gives us the tools to accomplish it. My dad narrated his story of leaving his ancestral village at an early age with nothing in his pocket. Now, God had made him a wealthy farmer, not because he was a better person than his neighbor, but because he had more work to do to help others find their role. God was expecting more from him than from the poorer neighbor. We are therefore all equal but very different, and we should embrace our differences as what makes us unique.

As I write this, I can still see his smile as he reflects on how awesome it is that God entrusted us with such responsibilities. I especially enjoyed when he explained to me his role as my father. God, the Almighty Father, handpicked him and entrusted him to be our caretaker here on earth. My father was to guide us and furnish us with the tools to find and carry out our purpose on earth.

My parents inside our local church in Munyenge,
after completing their premarital classes.

My parents on their Christian wedding day, in front of our local church in Munyenge.

Cocoa plants on my father's farm in the village of Munyenge.

Farmhouse where my father and I would rest, or stay the night, while drying the cocoa beans.

Hardworking farmers returning from their farms.

This is called an oven. We spent days on the farm drying
and roasting cocoa beans after harvesting.

CHAPTER 3

EARLY EDUCATION

MY PARENTS NEVER RECEIVED a formal education, but they believed in giving their children and other less fortunate children the best education available in the country. Following the British system of education, we started primary school at the age of six, or when we could physically reach across our head with the right hand and touch our left ear. Since most kids born in the villages had no official record of their birth, this is how the parents and school headmasters determined that a child was ready to start school. After six or seven years of primary school, and successfully passing a national certification examination, you would advance to secondary school. Secondary schools were classified as government (public) schools, or private secondary schools. Private schools were usually run by Catholic or Baptist missions. Private schools were more expensive and were typically attended by children of the affluent Cameroonians, government officials, or businessmen. The private schools generally were more structured than the public secondary schools. In the southwest region of Cameroon at that time, the most prestigious and expensive school was Saint Joseph's College, with its campus in the mountain village of Sasse, near the provincial capital of Buea. It was called Sasse College by the locals.

Sasse College was founded in 1939 by the St. Joseph's Missionary Society of Mill Hill Catholic missionaries under authority from the colonial master of the then-British territory of Southern Cameroon. It was the first English speaking secondary school in British Cameroon. I had completed primary school and passed the exit exams, and on merit, was ready for secondary school. In 1988, Saint Joseph's College, Sasse, was under the control of the Diocese of Buea, but it was being run by a non-clergy principal appointed by the bishop. It was an all-male boarding school. Not even female teachers worked there at that time. Once admitted, a student stayed on campus for the rest of the semester, only going home during the Christmas or summer breaks. There were occasional daily outings for students to replenish school supplies.

My father had heard about this school and was determined to get me there. A good friend of his had a son there, a senior, who could keep an eye on me. With the help of our local priest, we went through the application process. A few weeks later, when the list of students who were offered admission came out, we were notified by the priest that I was not accepted. Dad was disappointed. Three other children in my village who had performed well on their exit exams as well were also rejected. Their parents enrolled them in the nearby public school. Dad reached out to one of my uncles who lived in Buea and had attended the private school, but my uncle wasn't forthcoming.

A month before school was to begin, I still didn't know if I would be going to secondary school. All my primary school classmates whose parents could afford to send them to school already knew their fate. Not me. One morning, Dad woke me up at 3 a.m. and told me to get ready. We were going to visit the school principal. Dad's pickup truck was down so we had to get public transportation to Sasse. Using a flashlight in the darkness of the night, we started walking before getting picked up by a truck driver outside our village. We sat on the back of the open flatbed and hung on for dear life while the driver drove on rugged, volcanic rocky terrain to the next village. Several times I thought this would be my last day on earth. Dad was very quiet, but I could hear him murmur under his breath. He was rehearsing his speech for the principal.

We got to Sasse at about one in the afternoon, but the principal was at lunch. We sat on the floor in front of his office and waited. We were both covered in mud, as we had walked two miles from the truck drop-off to the school in the hot, rainy, and humid tropical weather. When Dad heard the principal walking towards us, he quickly stood up and asked me to stand at attention to impress the principal. The very well-dressed gentleman walked past us while Dad tried to introduce himself. Without ever looking in our direction, he asked Dad what he wanted. Dad asked if he could come in. The principal said "no" and again demanded what he wanted. My father reached into his bag, grabbed my primary school report cards, and asked the principal why I was not admitted. Without looking at my transcript, the principal told Dad that the school was very expensive and that most farmers could not afford it. Father asked about the cost. I can't remember how much the principal quoted. Father again reached in his bag and grabbed another plastic bag, full of money. He handed the principal the bag and told him that it was one year's worth of tuition and fees. He then dropped on his knees and said he would sell one of his farms and pay the entire five years of my secondary education.

Dad pleaded that I was an intelligent kid and needed a chance. After the principal told Dad to stand, he took us to the registrar's office where I was offered a spot in the incoming class. This event would repeat itself several times when my father would try to get my sisters and other relatives into private schools. On our way home, I asked him if he was afraid. "No," he responded angrily. He said that as a farmer in Cameroon with no education, a man would face class discrimination, abuse by government officials to extort money, and all sorts of prejudice on a daily basis. "You get no respect," he said. He wanted me to go to Sasse so that I wouldn't have to face the challenges he had faced.

All my life, I had seen my father as the ultimate caretaker who was never afraid of anyone. To see him on his knees begging on my behalf was a sight I have never been able to erase out of my head.

My first day of secondary school in Sasse was a major culture shock, even in my own country. I had spent my entire life in my small farming village with people who were just like me. I had never been to any town bigger than my village, except Muyuka. Now, at age eleven, I was about to leave my family. I would be able to see them again only during the holidays. My mother had spent the past month working on a list of mandatory items we needed to bring to school. In addition to the basic school supplies like pens, pencils, and erasers, we also needed to bring items like a machete to cut the grass and shrubs on the school grounds, as well as a broom made of palm branches to sweep clean the floors of our dorms, classrooms and living quarters. These items had to be stored in a metal box and a wooden locker next to our bunk beds in the dormitories. My mother was able to buy these items from the local market, but as she had for my sisters before me, she hand-tailored my uniforms. One of my uncles, a carpenter, designed and built my locker.

The morning of opening day, we got up very early. It would take us about two hours to make it to the town of Muyuka in my father's farm truck, and another three hours from Muyuka to Buea and then to Sasse. There were groups of kids who seemed to know each other running around and getting acquainted. It seemed everyone was well-dressed and very educated. Everyone spoke English or French. My dad looked confused and completely out of his element. He couldn't speak English, nor could he read the signs. Another parent helped us find my assigned dormitory. We found out that my dormitory was still another half a mile away, up a steep hill on a farm road leading from behind the main campus. It was called St. Augustine's Hall, and was one of the most remote dormitories from the school. By the time we made it to the dorm and got situated, I was late for dinner in the cafeteria. A senior student told my father to send me to the school cafeteria or I was going to miss dinner.

When we got back to the main campus, most of the cars had gone and it was getting dark. I looked for any reason to get my father to stay with me a little longer, but he had a long drive back home. I began crying and begging him not to leave me there. I was clinging to his leg, but he pulled me off and tried to console me by telling me that he was about the same age when he left his family. He assured me that the school administration would take good care of me. He couldn't have been more wrong. In any case, I went to the cafeteria to find out that I was too late, and dinner had already been served. Thankfully, I had some snacks that Mom had packaged to hold me over until breakfast. I must have cried all night.

We were awakened by the senior students before dawn the next day and asked to get our machetes to start trimming the grass that had covered the grounds around our dormitory while the students were on the summer break. This was the beginning of our boot camp and, quite honestly, the most miserable year of my life. One major mistake I made was showing off how good I was with the machete clearing thick, tall brush. This mistake would haunt me throughout the school year and would be one of the reasons my dad would transfer me out of this school to a different boarding school farther away from home. Between doing chores for senior students and clearing the grass almost daily, my palms were always covered in blisters. I felt more like a second-class farm laborer than a privileged student.

St. Joseph's College, Sasse had produced some of the most brilliant minds in Cameroon. I know many others who have great stories of their experiences there. I was not that fortunate. I felt like a fish out of water just struggling to catch my breath every day. The environment was so different from what I was used to in my village. Maybe it was because I missed my family, or it was the colder climate, but I was constantly physically sick. I spent a lot of time in the sick bay or infirmary. The infirmary was a small stand-alone building situated between the main dormitories and the school chapel. The nurse-doctor was a senior student who was handpicked by the school administration, probably for his science or medical inclination. He had no formal medical education whatsoever. When someone was sick, he would examine you and decide if your parents needed to be called, or if you should be taken to the hospital. There were beds where sick students would stay for observation. As a patient there, I observed many parents pick up their kids to take them to the hospital. Calling my parents wasn't an option since they couldn't be reached at their remote location and they lacked electricity or telephone, which made it impossible. My situation became quite desperate during a period called "handing over." This was after the school elections when the upper sixth students (12th grade) transfer authority to the lower sixth students (11th grade). Handing over had been considered the rite of passage. The lower sixth students who had been there six years get their chance to rule over the younger students. When I say rule, I mean military-styled ruling. There were morning drills, punishments for different reasons such as arriving late to class, or talking during bedtime or study periods. They could make up any reason for punishment. The most common form of punishment was brutal beating with sticks and belts. At times they even made students crawl on their knees on volcanic rocks and concrete walkways. If you didn't have a senior student to protect you, you would wish you were dead. It was that serious.

I had a few things going against me. I had no protection. There were a few senior students I knew, but they either weren't able to help or they too were blinded by the tradition. The more affluent schoolmates escaped the brutal punishments. I, on the other hand, could never catch a break. I went from one punishment to another with no time left to study. There were several occasions where I was punished because I was too weak to complete a task, especially during morning drills. I would fall on the ground and several students would beat me and force me to keep going.

Finally, one morning I was too tired to wake up. I had spent a couple of nights in a row doing chores for senior students, like washing their clothes, and I didn't hear the morning bell ring. A senior student who slept below me in our bunk bed kicked me. I landed on the concrete floor. I was convinced that I had fractured my back or my arm because I was in pain for days, but I had no time to worry about that. I had to keep going. Eventually, I got so sick that I seriously thought I was going to die. I reached out to a senior student whom I had found out was distantly related to me. His name was Celestine. His uncle lived in Limbe and was married to one of my mother's half-sisters. When Celestine saw me, he became very concerned about my health. He couldn't reach my parents and didn't have the money to take me to the hospital. So he came up with a plan to get me out of the school to someone who could help. I told him that I had an uncle in the nearby town of Buea. Celestine knew the van driver who delivered bread to school several times a week. They were both from the town of Limbe and had been neighbors. The driver offered to help. The driver usually arrived very early in the mornings, and would drop off the truckload of bread we ate for breakfast, and then leave, all before dawn. I was in the sick bay, so the next day he came to the sick bay very early in the morning and got me ready for the journey. After delivering the bread, the driver came and picked us both up.

Our first stop was Buea, but my uncle wasn't home. Celestine didn't want to leave me alone, so he asked the driver to take me to the police station in Limbe on his way home. Celestine's uncle was the senior commissioner of police for this station. I sat in the lobby of the police station until he arrived. Upon seeing me, he asked his police officers to help me into his car and took me to the Limbe General hospital. I was diagnosed with severe malaria and was very anemic. I was immediately admitted and started on IV fluids and antimalarial medications. I never knew if Celestine ever got permission from the administration to take me off campus, but I didn't care at that point. I just needed help. Eventually I would spend a few days with my aunt before heading back to school. It seemed no one even knew I had been gone for almost a week. My parents still didn't know, either. They would only find out during our break.

Another event that drove me from the school was the death on campus of a student I was very fond of. He, too, was from Limbe. He was a few years older than I, and three classes ahead of me. He was from my tribe, and his dad was the brother of one of my father's friends in the village. My father was relieved to find out that the fellow villager's nephew was in the same dormitory as me. He kept an eye on me and was always helpful when I needed anything. Though I knew him during the "handing over" period, he couldn't help my situation as he too was still two years from being a ruling upperclassman. Also, he was part of our school band that had been invited to perform off-campus. After the performance, on their way back to school, the band's driver lost control of the bus as it was climbing a steep hill on the campus, going toward the administration building. The bus rolled over backwards and left several students injured. My friend was apparently at the very back of the bus, by the window, and was either ejected or tried to get out but was pinned down under the bus. Several senior students, including Celestine, heard the accident, rushed to the scene and tried to lift up the vehicle. It was too late for my friend. A parent who was visiting their child at school took him in his car and rushed him to a nearby hospital. The news of his injuries spread.

We all went to bed at the normal lights-out time, only to be awakened by the sound of church bells at around midnight with instructions to go to the school chapel. That had never happened before, so we knew it was bad. When we got to the chapel, I noticed a stretcher on the middle aisle of the church facing the altar. On it was my friend's lifeless body draped with a bloodstained white bedsheet. The school priest, teachers and all the school administrators were present for a very sorrowful night vigil in his honor. His body was then transported to his family home in Limbe for the burial. We talked about him throughout the rest of that school year, but his passing was a major loss to me. One of the shadows that looked over me was suddenly gone. At my age of eleven, I just couldn't handle the feelings of emptiness and despair.

At the end of the school year, I went home with an average report card. I was promoted to the next class, but my experiences were so traumatic that I wasn't interested in going back to school. Not only Sasse, but any school. My dad knew something was not right from my grades, but I couldn't tell him the truth for two reasons: first, I still vividly remembered what he went through to get me into this school, and I never wanted to see him in that position again; secondly, I was afraid he would go to the school and confront the administration which might not be well received. The administration and students might retaliate against me if I were to return to the school. So I turned to my favorite uncle, John Atabong. He is now called Nkem, a title given to him by our traditional ruler. The title means advisor to the chief or king. Nkem is my mother's little brother. He was born about the time my father went to bring my mother from her home to their marital home. My grandfather was so impressed by my father that he named Nkem, John Atabong, after my dad.

When he was very young, my mother took him out of Fontem to get him his primary school education on the coast. He was about ten years older than me, so I always thought he was my big brother—not an uncle. I followed him everywhere, like his little sidekick. He had been against me going to Sasse initially, but in favor of another mission school called Seat of Wisdom College in Fontem, the town where my parents were born. Nkem finally convinced me to show my dad the fresh scars on my back from the lashes I received in Sasse. My dad was furious, but Mom persuaded him that going to the school to talk to the principal would not make any difference. Nkem would use this opportunity to talk my parents into transferring me to Seat of Wisdom. My father was very worried about me being that far away from home after the experience I had in Sasse, but Nkem and my mother assured him that my mother's sisters would keep an eye on me. There was also a hospital with a doctor, owned by the same mission that owned the school. My little sister, Clementine, had also been admitted to the same school. She would be coming in as a ten-year-old form-one student and me a twelve-year-old form-two student. Nkem promised my parents that he would personally take us and make sure that we were well situated before he came back home.

Despite those assurances, I didn't want to go. Nkem spent the entire summer telling me stories about Fontem and how much fun it would be to travel with him. He promised to buy me anything I wanted on our way to Fontem, including roadside meals. He was very convincing, so I agreed to go with him. I wasn't even admitted to the school yet, but he was sure he could get me in. One of my older sisters had graduated from there as the senior prefect—that is, student council president. He was confident that he could use this argument to get me admitted. Once again, I would embark on yet another journey to secondary school. This time I was taking my uncle's word for it. I was somewhat excited because I wasn't going back to Sasse, and because my little sister and I would be traveling together.

The journey was more treacherous than I had anticipated. We traveled on the back of a pickup truck from Munyenge to Muyuka. We waited at the motor park for hours for the taxi driver to fill up his tiny Toyota Tercel with passengers before he would depart for our next stop, the town of Kumba. When it was time to go, they packed us in the Toyota like sardines in a can. My uncle had paid a full fare for us, but because we were so little the driver made us sit between other passengers. I was placed in the front between the driver and two other passengers on my right. I sat on the utility console with one leg on the driver's side, and the other leg on the passenger side with the gear shift between my legs. The car had a manual transmission. My seat did not have a back rest, so I rested my head on the hand luggage of a very nice lady sitting behind me. As soon as we took off I fell asleep only to be awakened every two minutes or so by either the woman adjusting my head from the back, or the driver moving my leg to change gears as he drove along. In Kumba, my uncle bought us our first roadside meal at the motor park as we waited another couple of hours for our next ride. This time it was a four-wheel-drive Toyota pickup.

I thought we had the worst roads in my hometown, but the road from Kumba to Fontem trumped anything I had ever experienced. The road to Munyenge was rugged, but at least it was all volcanic rocks. The Kumba-to-Fontem road was red clay. In the rainy season it became very muddy. To make it even worse, we were driving on the side of steep hills and mountains. My uncle kept telling us not to look out into the valleys. We stopped several times to help other cars and passengers who had gotten stuck in the mud or stranded. Some had been there for days.

Our passenger four-wheel-drive pickup truck made it just outside the village of Fontem but couldn't climb the final hill into the village, so the driver told us we would have to trek up the hill. By then, we had been traveling for more than eighteen hours. So my uncle went into a nearby bush and cut out some leaves. He asked some passengers to help put both our metal suitcases on his head, and used the leaves as a cushion. My little sister started crying because she was tired and hungry, and couldn't make it to the top of the hill. So, in the middle of the night, with two suitcases on his head, my uncle stooped and asked my sister to get on his back. He carried her and I followed them up the hill to the first government outpost of Menji where we would spend whatever was left of that night on the floor of the council building. The next morning, we went to one of our relatives' home to get ready for the first day of school. When my uncle took me to Seat of Wisdom for admission, the principal was very concerned. She knew of the reputation of Sasse students and was worried that I would corrupt her students with the Sasse tradition of bullying and brutality against the younger students. After a very long assurance, and thankful for my older sister's almost-perfect academic record, I was admitted on a one-year trial basis. I spent the next four years at Seat of Wisdom.

I made long-lasting friends at the school and was exposed to what I consider the most productive form of charity, one that was based on helping people with their health and education in a manner that allowed them to eventually be independent. This charity was focused on the right of every child to learn in an environment that protected their dignity and nurtured their body and their minds.

I quickly became quite popular, thanks to my favorite aunt, O'Amin, my mother's eldest sister, who lived about a mile from the campus. Her birth name is Aminkeng, but we called her O'Amin, one of the highest forms of maternal respect in my dialect. O'Amin was never able to bear any children, but she treated us as her own. She always referred to me as "Papa" because I was also named after my grandfather, her father. She told me that my smile and mannerism reminded her of her father who passed away before I moved to Seat of Wisdom. She unfailingly visited us every Saturday with home-cooked meals which we typically shared with our friends. I believe my little sister and I received more visits than any other student in the school. Everyone wanted to be our friend, especially for the weekly meals that my aunt brought us.

The best part about transferring from Sasse College to Seat of Wisdom College was the girls. I left an all-male institution to come to one that was coeducational. When you put 500-plus teenage boys and girls together in a confined space with a zero tolerance for dating, you end up with some very adventurous stories. The rules were simple: there was absolutely no touching of the opposite sex in any way or form that might be seen as romantic. If you were caught, it was grounds for immediate dismissal.

By my fourth year, I had become somewhat popular among the girls. I had been elected the assistant senior prefect, the equivalent of the vice president of the student council, and stayed among the top five percentile of my class. Best of all, I had been appointed the team captain for my soccer team, and we pulled off an amazing victory against our arch-rival school, which we hadn't beaten in years. I had it all—the perfect recipe for a disastrous end.

With this new-found status, I somehow ended up dating a girl that we boys, at the time, considered the prettiest on campus. She was smart, funny, well-liked by all, and most importantly for me, a village boy, she was from the big city of Douala. I was dating a rich city girl. She and I were both ready to take our relationship to the next level, which, to us, was kissing. Just kissing, that's it. My attempt at getting my first kiss is still today considered one of the biggest scandals on campus. The sheer number of friends and time it took to plan this production was itself Academy Award-worthy. To execute, it would take the entire student body. The plan: During "social night," with all the student assembled in the social hall, she would excuse herself from the hall to meet a friend waiting outside. Another friend ensured that no other student left the hall during the twenty-to-thirty minutes this plan would require. There were two other students stationed in strategic locations to watch for approaching administrators. They were to signal us by whistling, which meant to abandon the plan.

The girl would then be handed over to another friend who would bring her to my location, the darkest spot behind my class. Everything went perfectly until we got caught right before the kiss. We didn't factor in the loud, fast-flowing river behind my class, which prevented us from hearing the campus security guard, Mr. Isaac, quietly walking toward us. My eyes closed,

going in for the kiss, I could see light through my eyelids. It was
Mr. Isaac's flashlight pointed right at our faces. Almost thirty
years later, I still get questions from my schoolmates who are
curious how I managed not to get expelled from the school—or
how I kept it a secret from my father. Everyone knew well that
if my father had found out that I even thought about kissing, it
surely would have been the end of my life. I would later find out
after graduation that the principal was told of the incident, but
she decided not to expel me. We students walked around campus
for months, thinking that we were on our way out. The principal
never said a word to me. For the longest time, I thought Mr.
Isaac had taken pity on us and never told the principal. I never
got the chance to thank the principal personally or understand
why she chose to allow me to stay, because sadly she passed
away in 2001 from a motor vehicle accident.

Because Seat of Wisdom did not yet have a high school in
1993, I would go back to Sasse College for my final two years.
This time, the decision was all mine. I had overcome my fears
and was mature enough to know how to handle anything that
came my way. I would also be coming in as a lower sixth student,
which meant I wouldn't be going through the bullying that the
younger students endured. Thankfully, when I got there, I was
pleased to find out that Sasse had a new principal who was also
a priest. He was slowly doing away with the "handing over"
traditions. It also helped when I found out that my girlfriend
from Seat of Wisdom was planning on attending an all-girls high
school in the Buea area after her graduation. I was hoping to
finally get that kiss.

The last two years were uneventful, except that my girlfriend
would leave me for one of my classmates. Her reasons, detailed
in a three-page handwritten letter, were simple—I was poor and
not sophisticated enough for her. Like most teenagers after a
breakup like this, I thought it was the end of the world. I was
heartbroken and needed a place far away to forget about her and
her new boyfriend. Where I found myself next would turn out to
be the most unlikely destination for a kid like me.

At the airport in Douala in 2016, I had a chance encounter with two previous principals from Seat of Wisdom College, Miss Clalia from Italy (left) and Mr. Nelson from Brazil.

At Seat of Wisdom College, I cleaned the graves of two Focolare Movement volunteers who died while serving in Fontem.

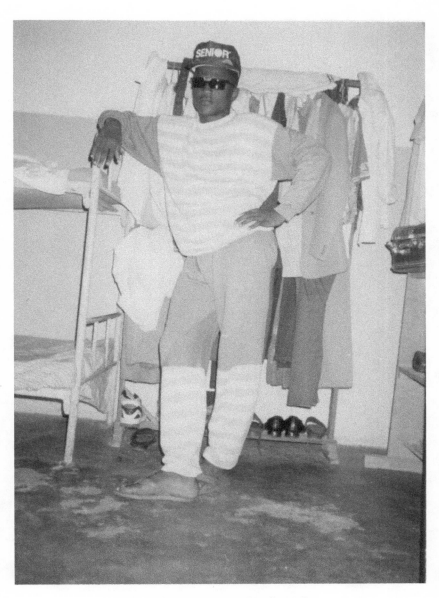

Me in my dormitory at Seat of Wisdom College.

My elder sister and I visited Seat of Wisdom for its 50th anniversary celebration. Here we stand with the previous principal, Mr. Nelson from Brazil.

Seat of Wisdom College, Fontem.

St. Joseph's College, Sasse.

Transporting passengers from Munyenge to Muyuka today.

CHAPTER 4

COMING TO AMERICA

THE IDEA OF MOVING to America had never crossed my mind because I never thought that was even a possibility for someone of my background. I did get pretty good exposure to people at St. Joseph's College Sasse who had visited or planned to travel to the US. It was one of the favorite destinations for our most privileged families. We had several children of ministers and high-ranking government officers or businessmen who would usually send their kids overseas for Christmas or summer holidays. After spending my holidays farming in the village, I always looked forward to returning to school to hear stories from these schoolmates about their recent overseas adventures. They had stories of their airplane flights, the cities they had visited, the foods they consumed, and the life of luxury everywhere they went. I am sure they found my barrage of questions annoying.

At night I would lie in my bed, put all the stories together in my head and live their lives in my fantasy world. I would then snap out of my dream and tell myself that maybe, if I became successful in farming, I could possibly send my children to study in the US, as there is no possible way my father could afford an overseas education. Maybe I could study in Nigeria, or if my father's farm did well, I could go to South Africa. But Europe or the US was out of the question.

Prior to my year of departure, my father and I never had discussed my studying abroad. The few times that I would attempt to tell him stories or things I studied about America, he would yell at me and tell me to stop dreaming and concentrate instead on what was important and possible. He would give me lectures on worrying about things I could control, such as making good grades each year, clearing the grass on the farm, and making sure we did everything possible to guarantee a bountiful harvest. Again, he would use his farm to educate me on being goal-oriented.

On a typical cocoa farm, the farmer worked year-round. It took years for a plant to start producing, after it was planted. During this growing phase you had to protect the plant from weeds and bushes by keeping the area clear of dry leaves, insects and parasites. The plants might be destroyed by drought or heavy rain, but my father would say these are things that are beyond your control, and humans have no business worrying about them. He would say that anyone who worries about these natural disasters easily gets distracted and loses focus on the task at hand, or they are looking for excuses for a way out. On the other hand, if you go a year without your crops being destroyed by the things you cannot control, and you did all you were supposed to do, you shall have an excellent product.

Applying this basic concept would give you full control of your destiny. Dad would use this same principle to teach us about setting achievable goals on almost any task, including studying abroad. As I would find out later, his goals for my life included me studying in America, but this plan would evolve over time and he always had full control of it from the day I was born. My only part of this was to deliver the grades that would make this goal achievable.

Anyone who paid Pa Atabong a visit at his home in Munyenge knew of his small, rusted battery-powered Sharp radio given to him as a gift in the early 1970s. Back then, the stations he could receive were the government controlled, including the British Broadcasting Corporation, BBC. The only program on the national radio station he was interested in was the national news at 2 PM daily, but the BBC covered the world news 24/7. So he would usually listen to the local news during work breaks, and spend evenings after work and on weekends listening to BBC. Through his interactions with people during his days working at the plantation in Meanja and Muyuka, he picked up an understanding of the English language, though he couldn't read or write. While listening to BBC, he would frequently ask us children what was being said or what something meant. Most of the time we did not understand it either, which irritated Dad because he worked hard to send us to school so we could understand. Since I was usually with him on the farm, I would make up explanations to avoid disappointing him.

His favorite news items were individual success stories such as Margaret Thatcher, Britain's first female prime minister, and stories about Michael Jackson and his acceptance around the world. He was also inspired by Martin Luther King, Jr., Mother Theresa, Mahatma Gandhi, John F. Kennedy, and Pope John Paul II. He believed that America was the best country that offered the most opportunity for success to someone starting off without money, influence or power, but having the right moral compass and ability to work hard. He also understood that it would take time and sacrifice on his part, and maybe not be his first child, but one of his children would make a success in the United States.

The first opportunity for one of us to travel to the US ended badly and was a devastating blow to my father and our family. No one in my village had ever been to the States, but in a nearby city there was a very successful family that had sent their son to study there in the 1980s. Their son was interested in pursuing a relationship with one of my sisters.

One summer evening, we were visited by the son's parents wanting to talk to my parents. Their son somehow knew my sister and had been communicating with her. They were asked by their son to come and ask my parents for her hand in marriage. My father was very good at keeping secrets, but by the next morning the entire village knew of the marriage proposal. Everyone also knew that my sister had accepted without ever meeting this guy. All that mattered was that the son was an American.

Arrangements were made for the families to start putting together all the documents, as he would be visiting Cameroon soon and most likely taking my sister to the US embassy to apply for a visa. Just based on this simple development, the status of both families shot through the roof. For my family, it was simple—one of my sisters would be marrying into one of the most influential, best-educated and wealthiest families in the region. For the other family it was a little more complicated. At the time my father had more children than any other monogamous family in the village. He had five beautiful daughters. Most boys in the village wanted to date my sisters but were deathly afraid of my father who was very strict and absolutely against any form of dating before marriage. This meant that we never left the house without permission or an escort. So, for about a year before this young man visited Cameroon, my parents made it well known that she was "off the market."

The next summer the young man visited my family in the village. The son was well dressed and very respectful to my parents. With all the trust built up by his family, my parents for the first time agreed to let my sister travel to meet members of his family before making arrangements to take her to the US. This brief engagement lasted for about a week before the gentleman finally returned to the US with the promise to start making wedding plans and collecting all necessary documents for her to travel and join him. Months went by after his return to the US with no correspondence from him and just an occasional visits from his parents to assure my parents that their son was still making arrangements.

A year went by and the visits stopped. Then stories started coming in from people in the US indicating that he was already involved in another relationship in the US and had no intention of marrying my sister. Then came the dreadful confirmation from his parents that he was getting married to someone else. I was present during the visit. I couldn't hear what they were saying but could tell that both fathers were disappointed. Over the years, my father went from anger to frustration, then to depression. He later told me that he wasn't mad at the young man or his parents, but at himself for letting his guard down and permitting his daughter to travel with this man unsupervised. Had the young man taken advantage of my sister's trust and vulnerability during his visit to Cameroon? I don't think he and my sister ever talked about the suitor again.

My sister eventually got married, but the relationship between the two families was never the same again. My father also told me that after this incident he heard countless stories of this happening to other families: well-educated men from the States would travel to Cameroon and make promises to marry young girls, spend time with the girls but never return for them. He said the families of the girls were usually uneducated and poor and hence vulnerable to such things.

Initially, Dad thought this reprehensible behavior must have been something they learned in America, and therefore rejected the idea of me going to the US for fear I would become like one of those boys. For years he wouldn't even allow us to talk about anything American. Then one afternoon on the farm, he confessed to me that he disliked America but realized that if he didn't get his children out of our current environment, we would never know any better and my children would be vulnerable to the same situation. He understood that every parent wanted their child to study or travel to the US because it provided the best chance of success for even the poorest kids, if they were willing to work hard. He then looked at me and promised me he would do everything in his power to make sure I got an American education; in return, he made me promise that I would never treat a girl or her family the way these "American boys" had treated our family and my sister. I was sixteen and it was the first time my father would permit me to start dreaming again about going to America.

There would be many failed attempts by my dad to get me to the US. At the time, there were scam artists who found the farmers to be easy targets because of their lack of education and inability to verify information. These scammers usually came to the village during the harvest season, after the farmers had just sold their crops and had cash. In my last two years of high school, Dad would be exploited by these scams several times. The first was by a gentleman whose parents lived not too far from us. He was selling life and education insurance and worked for an American life insurance company. He had all the proper documents and successfully sold my parents life insurance that would take care of all our needs on their passing. He also sold them insurance that would pay for our education no matter where we went to school. My dad became suspicious when he found out that one family went to the head office of this company in Douala, only to find out that the guy neither worked for the company nor did he buy any insurance products from them. He sent the documents to a family member in Douala who confirmed we were the victims of a scam.

My dad's next encounter was with a man who visited my family after watching me play soccer for my high school. He said he was a scout representing several US schools. After watching me, he found a school in the US that wanted me to come play on a full scholarship, and the only thing my parents had to do was pay for my visa application and my airline ticket to the US. After seeing all his fake credentials my parents shelled out two million CFA francs (about $4,000), which was an enormous proportion of their yearly harvest. The "scout" took the money, left and was never seen again.

I was a year away from graduating and so far, every chance to study in the US had been a scam. My parents started preparing for me to attend university in Cameroon. They were very reluctant to do this, as every child who went to university came back after graduation with no job. My last chance to get to the US would come six months before my graduation from a very unlikely source. In January of 1995, while I was preparing for my final national certification examination, I received an unusual visit from my brother-in-law. He was sent by my parents to come get my transcripts. He explained to me that one of my uncles who worked for the United Nations was sending his son to study in America. They had many other families in mind, but if my father could come up with $16,000 within two months, they would start my application process. I looked at my brother-in-law with anxiety and asked where in the world my dad would get that type of money. My brother in-law knew that if anyone could make miracles happen, it would be my father, but he was also very skeptical. He had a long visit with my father and they discussed options, most of which involved borrowing money to pay back over years. They didn't know anyone who had that type of money or was willing to lend such a large sum to a farmer. They both went to bed that night disappointed. My brother-in-law, who was travelling back to the city, was awakened at 4 AM by my dad who said he would come up with the money. He told my uncle to proceed with the application. My brother-in-law, knowing my father's word was good, knew that was all he needed to travel to my high school to collect my transcripts.

My father had decided he would sell his oldest, largest and most productive cocoa farm so he could send me to America. When he told me this, my jaw dropped. I grew up on this farm and everything we owned came from years of hard labor by my parents to send us to good schools and provide us with a decent living. If he sold the farm, my parents might not have enough money to support the rest of the family. Not to mention, this would only pay for a year of college. What about the three years after that? I had the chance to ask my dad these questions during a short break from school. His response was that he trusted I would study so hard or be so good at soccer that the Americans would find a way of keeping me. And if not, he has given me all the tools to survive by myself on nothing. He sent me back to school with the promise that he would take care of everything and for me to study hard and make him proud.

My last few months of school were very difficult. I would cry several times out of guilt that my parents were sacrificing everything for me. I hardly slept. I had nightmares: what if the money is paid and I don't get accepted? What if I travel but don't do well? What if I run out of money and get sent back?

My cousin was calm and collected. He had visited several countries before. His life was certain. We were given permission from school on two occasions to go have physical examinations and collect documents for my visa application. At the same time, we had to keep this a secret from our friends and classmates. I finally received the news that I had been accepted by the same university as my cousin, and we would be travelling together. It was hard for me to contain my excitement. After taking my final examinations, I was picked up by my brother-in-law who was taking me to the village to say goodbye to my family. I didn't know anything about my flight or travel arrangements. I was told that my father had paid for my flight and tuition for an entire year at a university in Arkansas. I would pack my favorite shoes and clothes in a small bag, but was to leave everything else behind.

My sisters had already prepared my favorite meal. They were already calling me their American brother. We ate, talked, laughed and cried all night long. We had all been together since we were born, and at age eighteen I was leaving my hometown to go to a strange land. The most interesting part was that my father, knowing that this was my last day, came back from the farm very late. He ate dinner with us, but said very little. After dinner, he called us all into the living room and gave us one last speech centered on respecting everyone I meet as God's creation. He said to treat everyone I meet as I would like to be treated, never forget where I came from, and come back to help the people in my community. He tried several times to hold back tears and did a great job. I, on the other hand, could not stop crying out loud, especially when Dad said he didn't know how long before we would see each other again, so if he passed before my return, to take good care of my mom and siblings. He then took me to the edge of my village and showed me a piece of land that he had bought several years ago. He wanted me to use the land to build a hospital someday.

When we got back home, he told me that he would not be able to make it to the international airport in Douala to see me off. That night my sisters all insisted on sleeping in the same room with me. We fell asleep in the living room with some of us on the floor. I was awakened at 5 AM by my father calling me into his room to give me his last words. After re-iterating his speech from the previous night, he did a traditional blessing by covering his mouth with his palms, blew his breath into his hands and rubbed my face saying, "Go in peace." He then picked up his farm tools and left.

My brother-in-law was ready to drive us to Douala. I said an emotional goodbye to my mom and siblings and we got into his car and left. I would see Mom again two weeks later at the airport to see me off. I spent the next two weeks in Douala being reminded by my sister of the sacrifices our parents had made for me, and their expectations. My sister said no one thought my dad would raise the $16,000 needed for me to attend college in America. But that had changed one Sunday morning when her doorbell rang. She opened the door and my dad stood there, covered in mud, with the same traditional bag he had taken to pay my tuition in Saint Joseph's College Sasse, wrapped over his shoulder. He had sold the farm and received the money the day prior. He saw a truck transporting farm produce to Douala and paid them to take him there. Douala is a very big city and, though he had a general idea of where my sister lived, he did not know the exact address. So he had asked the driver to drop him off at an intersection and he would walk the rest of the way, since there were no taxis that late. He got lost several times but found my sister's house after walking three miles; he couldn't read the signs and refused to ask for directions for fear of running into thieves.

My sister said my dad immediately handed the bag to her and told her this was the money for my travel. My sister was so shocked that she threw the bag to the ground after seeing the bundles of money. She demanded to know where my dad got the money before she would let him into her house. This is how she found out that my dad had sold the farm to a businessman for far less than it was worth.

The day for me to travel finally arrived. Of everyone in the house, the only one that had ever been on a plane was my brother-in-law, who tried to tell my Mom and my oldest sister that airlines would not allow food. Well, the ladies didn't listen. They had spent the last two weeks baking and smoking enough food to last me a whole year. They had fried fish, beef jerky, goat jerky, and anything that they thought could survive thirty-plus hours without refrigeration. All these packaged enough to sustain a hurricane. On the day of the flight, we met my uncle's wife and my cousin at the airport. My mom insisted that we go to the airport four hours before the flight in case the pilot decided to depart two hours prior to the scheduled time because, back home, she was used to using passenger cars in the village where the drivers would leave as soon as they had a full passenger load.

The airport was congested and the heat unbearable, but I was able to see my plane through the crowds. It was the only plane in the middle of a giant open space.

I still don't remember what airline it was. All I knew was that I was getting on a plane to travel to America. I had never seen a plane before. They all looked like large birds. How could something that big fly? I was downright scared. My mother was, too. I was standing beside her when she saw the plane for the first time. She screamed and grabbed my hands so tight as if to take me back home. Our emotional roller coaster was interrupted when my aunt and cousin arrived. The next two hours went by very fast. My cousin was talking calmly and laughing at jokes; I wasn't. First, we went through passport checks, where the police officer, after seeing the anxiety in my face, tried to assure me that everything would be fine. The customs was the last checkpoint where my family could be with me. After this it would be just me, my cousin and my aunt supervising my every step. At this stop I was told I couldn't take all the food mom had prepared. We had to take out all the food and give it to my family to take home. My mother was devastated. This was her only way to ensure my survival. She realized that she would not be cooking for me anymore. The reality was hard for her to swallow. As a result, she told my aunt all my likes and dislikes and insisted that I was a picky eater. My aunt was irritated because she had told my family not to prepare any food. She nevertheless reassured my mom that my school had all the foods that I liked. I gave everyone a hug and proceeded to the next stop. Up to this point, every checkpoint had been with the Cameroonian authority.

Our next checkpoint was a white person who greeted me with a smile and asked how my day was going. I don't remember responding to her, figuring that she would soon realize that I was a farmer's son and therefore didn't deserve to go to America. To me, every person after the last checkpoint was American and each had the power to send me back. She looked at my passport and printed boarding pass. She handed it to me and said "Welcome on board." We had a few more checkpoints to go through, but I told myself that if I wasn't cleared she would not have welcomed me to the flight. We finally made it into the plane and my aunt showed me my seat. I had a window seat and from my window I could see the engine was already running. I turned and told my cousin that they had already started the plane and might have left without us. He smiled and said they keep the engine running all the time. I didn't understand why, but who was I to question him? I could also see the crowd on the balcony of the airport, waving goodbye. I tried but couldn't spot my mom but felt they were still waving goodbye.

It was a Friday and we took off at night, so I could not see any landmarks. But I could see the city of Douala slowly disappearing from beneath us. I very quickly fell asleep and when I awoke we were in Brazzaville, Congo. I looked out the window and thought we were back in Douala. The airport was similar to the one we left. I didn't see any white people. Still in my disoriented state, I heard my aunt tell me that we were here and needed to grab my bags. It turned out that we would join my uncle who worked in Brazzaville and stay for about a week. It was during this week that I would be going to the American embassy to apply for a visa. Since my uncle was officially my guardian, he would have to apply on my behalf. He picked us up at the airport and drove us to his house in a residential area of the capital city of Congo. I didn't speak a word and he knew I was worried. I had just left my home country of Cameroon and told my friends and family goodbye that I was going to America. Now I just found out that I didn't yet have a visa to travel to the US and would have to wait until Monday to find out my fate. *What if I didn't get a visa? Would I have to go back to Cameroon? Would I stay in Congo? What about my father's farm that he sold already? Does he know I am still in Africa? If so, why didn't he warn me not to get my hopes up as the most important hurdle was getting a visa?*

I had heard horror stories of people who have invested everything to travel only to get declined for a visa. As a matter of fact, everyone I knew at this point whose parents weren't wealthy were denied a visa. My weekend in Brazzaville, Congo, was a very emotional time for me. There were several activities planned— to go and see the city or visit my uncle's friends—but I opted to stay at home each time. I wasn't the only one who needed a visa, but no one else seemed concerned, as they had already been to the same embassy several times. On Monday morning, I was the first to wake up. I was dressed in my best attire and waiting in the living room when my uncle came out from his room. He informed me that he had a lot of work that morning and would not be accompanying us to the embassy. It would just be my cousin, my uncle's wife and me. I thought, *If he is my guardian, shouldn't he need to go explain that? What if they start asking me questions?* He told me that it would be okay. His driver drove us to the embassy and walked us in. The receptionist greeted us in French and asked my aunt how she had been. They visited for a few minutes then she handed our passports to the receptionist who left and came back a few minutes later and told us to come back that afternoon to pick up our visas. We left and drove to the local farmers' market to buy some food. We went back around 3 PM and there it was—my passport with an American visa in it. They didn't ask me a single question. I couldn't believe it. My aunt showed me my visa and assured me that I was going to America. I could feel the weight lift from my shoulders. My body felt incredibly light, but my heart was racing as if counting down for liftoff. I wanted to scream. I wanted to cry. I wanted to dance. But I couldn't, because no one else around me was fazed by this decision. It was the outcome they all expected.

On July 26, 1995, we would travel to the Brazzaville International Airport, but this time I was truly flying to America. The security checks were less stressful. This time I would see and remember that my flight was Swissair. The plane was much bigger than my first flight a week earlier. The flight attendant welcomed me and showed me to my seat. I fell asleep before we even took off. When I awoke we were in Zurich, Switzerland. Our next flight was to Atlanta, but this time I stayed awake during the entire flight, trying to make sense of what was happening to me. I already missed my family so much. I wished my sisters were with me to help me celebrate. I found myself repeating my father's last words and the promise I made to him. I had no idea what the future held for me. But in God's name and for the sacrifices my family made for me, I had no option but to succeed. I got a rush of energy right when the pilot announced we were ten minutes to landing and welcomed me to the United States of America.

A young boy on his way to the farm carrying cocoa insecticide and sprayer.

Final picture of me before I came to the US.

Me (back row, left) with my parents and siblings the day
before I departed for the United States.

My family performing a traditional blessing before my departure
from my village to travel to the U.S. Clock on the wall shows 4 a.m.

My father with his famous Sharp radio.

My sisters Hannah (left) and Mary (right) seeing me off at the Douala airport.
My mother is in the middle.

CHAPTER 5

FIRST YEAR
IN AMERICA

FROM THE MOMENT WE landed in Atlanta, I knew I was
in a different world. My first challenge was overcoming cultural
and language barriers. On our way to baggage claim, I was
impressed by the cleanliness and the size of the airport. It was
quiet, and everyone seemed to know where they were going.
My aunt's brother, Uncle George, picked us up in his Toyota
minivan, which was for private use. At home it would have been
a taxi. Every room in Uncle George's apartment had lights. The
entire house was carpeted. When dinner was served we could
eat whatever we wanted and if you couldn't finish your food, you
just threw it in the trash. I even had my own can of Coca-Cola.
I was told I could eat and drink as much as I wanted.

Growing up in my village, the only time I might have had a
bottle of Coca-Cola or a piece of chicken to myself was during
our annual Christmas feast. If I did, I typically would share that
bottle of Coke with friends who had come to wish us a Merry
Christmas. I would make that bottle of Coke or Fanta last all
day. My village in Cameroon never had electricity. Even my
sister's house, in the big city of Douala, had lights in just a few

rooms. She had one small window air conditioning unit that kept her and her husband's room cool. The rest of her house was without air conditioning. We had no running water in my village. We walked long distances to fetch for drinking water, and took our baths in rivers or springs fed by freezing waters from the mountains. We used the same water to cook and do our laundry.

My mother cooked our meals in a separate building to keep the smoke out of the house. Her fireplace was made up of three rocks placed diagonally to form a triangular stand where the cooking pot would be placed. Wood from our farms was our only source of fire. Our toilet was an outhouse or latrine located about fifty yards from behind our main house closer to the forest, to keep the smell of feces from the house. If I had to use the toilet at night, which happened frequently, I would have to wake up one of my older sisters to accompany me with a kerosene-powered bush lamp for light. It was always a scary ordeal. We were encouraged to use the toilet together before bedtime or, if we could hold it, until dawn. And if you had diarrhea, you were flat out screwed. You typically would not be able make it before having an accident. Everyone knew when you had diarrhea because of the speed at which you ran past them with your hands on your bottom.

At Uncle George's apartment in Atlanta, each room had air conditioning. There were multiple lightbulbs per room, and the lights were always on. They had running water coming out of the faucets. Uncle George had his own personal shower in his room and didn't have to take a bath in a pool of spring water in front many others, like we did in our village or the school dormitories. Here, you just dumped dirty clothes in a machine and hit a button and your laundry came out clean and scented. There was a toilet next to my bedroom. I remember the first time I asked for a broom to clean the house, they gave me a machine with detailed instructions on how to push the high-tech device around the house. No more machetes to clear the grass. Someone else does that for you, with a machine, of course. They cooked using an electric stove inside the same building. *Fire to cook without producing any smoke? Fascinating!* My poor mother could have definitely used this, as her eyes were always bloodshot from the smoke in her kitchen. I was in complete culture shock. The world as I knew it was flipped upside down. No one at home had a clue what I was experiencing. Nothing could have prepared me for my new American life. I compared everything in astonishment to my lifestyle in Africa.

Other than the news we got from my father's radio, and the stories from friends who may have visited the US, my understanding of the American system was based on what I was taught in secondary and high school. This was limited to the history and geography of the US. Even though I was a science student, I loved these other subjects because they gave me a glimpse of something other than my village. Life growing up in Munyenge was all I had ever known before secondary school. My favorite courses throughout secondary and high school were World Geography and World History. My favorite teacher taught both classes in secondary school. He was so charismatic and detailed, you would think he was actually present when the events happened, or had actually been to these places. One semester we were asked to do a case study on domestic policies of President Franklin D. Roosevelt.

In Cameroon, there were no multiple-choice exams. Questions were in essay format and if you did illustrations, you would get extra points. You had to study the entire book and understand the content. There was no room for guesswork. We studied and were expected to master the key domestic and foreign achievements of all American presidents from World War I to George H. Bush. My favorite American presidents were Franklin D. Roosevelt and John F. Kennedy. FDR's story was inspirational to me. He would survive poliomyelitis to become an American president and take the country out of the Great Depression. Even at a young age, I knew about polio and had seen people killed by the disease. My cousin Louis had been handicapped by it. I also knew that in my country, most handicapped people were left to fend for themselves, as the families could not afford to care for them. A great majority of them ended up begging on the streets. My father was very fond of Louis. He always insisted that he spend the summer holidays with us. Since Louis couldn't farm, my father would give him little chores around the house. At the end of summer, he would take him back to his family with money for his tuition and pocket money for the year. He didn't want Louis to stop going to school or end up on the streets.

During one of the final examinations at the end of the semester I got excited when I saw that one of the questions was about FDR. I raised my hand and asked for more paper to start writing my essay. I must have written five pages, including illustrations of the Hoover Dam, which I thought was his most important accomplishment in the New Deal. In my frame of reference, the Hoover Dam harnessed power from a fast-flowing river, just like the much smaller river at my dad's farm. I got a *C* grade because I spent half the test period drawing a picture of my dad's farm. I ignored the other 80 percent of the test that had to do with the history of Cameroon and the accomplishments of its president, who coincidentally had also picked the New Deal as his party's motto.

Prior to my travel to the US, my longest uninterrupted stay in a city was the few days I spent in my sister's home in Douala, which was a luxury. Now, I was in Atlanta for a week. During the day our host would leave for work, and I would get up and clean the house. My mother taught us to always show our appreciation for our host by always being the first ones to wake up and clean. After cleaning I would literally watch TV until they got back from work—there was nothing else to do. It was the most boring week of my life. We couldn't just go out and walk around the neighborhood in Atlanta like we did in the village at home.

I noticed my cousin was on the phone a lot. He told me he was calling his friends in Cameroon to tell them he had arrived safely. The only phone number I had was my sister's in Douala. He helped me dial her number and I spent hours on the phone talking to her and my nephews. We would later find out that we left our gracious host with a phone bill of around $1,000. I have never talked to them about this. I hope they have forgiven me.

From Atlanta we were off to Dallas to visit my aunt's sister Sophie. While in Dallas our host took us to my first experience of a Chinese buffet, a concept I still don't understand. For a set price you can eat as much food as your stomach could hold. And that's exactly what I did. I ate so much that I went to the restroom and vomited all of it. When I returned to the table, I was told that I might be getting sick and should go rest in the car. They handed me the keys and showed me where the car was parked. So I opened the car door, got in and fell asleep. When everyone joined me, they were convinced that I had malaria or typhoid because now I was running a fever and getting a little disoriented. But I think I got a heat stroke from falling asleep inside a car in the Dallas summer heat. I know this because I was perfectly fine the next day, after cooling off and hydrating that evening. After Dallas, we took the bus to Austin to visit my aunt's friend. Our last stop was Arkansas for my first semester of school.

My aunt got us situated in our new boarding school in Arkansas. Before she left, she took me to Walmart for school supplies. I got two pairs of shoes, one for the cold season which I was still to experience. She bought me my jacket as well. I had a $150 allowance in case I needed anything, but I was told that the money my father had paid covered my meals and everything else I needed for that entire school year. My aunt reminded me of the sacrifices my father had made for me, and encouraged me to make my father proud.

The school was predominantly white people. Fewer than 5 percent of the students were black, but I felt at home from day one. It almost seemed like the school authorities knew what we were going through, and so went out of their way to make us feel welcome. Most gracious were the citizens of this little college town in Arkansas. People would frequently offer to take us to church on Sundays and then out to lunch afterward. Occasionally, they would take us by Walmart before dropping us back at our dormitories.

My favorite family was the Hodges family. Mrs. Hodges worked as the secretary to the president of the university. She counseled me on every issue I had. She introduced me to all her kids, one of whom was a student at the university, and she made sure he checked on me. After each test, I would go over to her office to show her my grades. She was so genuinely proud of me and would encourage me always to keep it up. My roommate was from another town in Arkansas. He was very nice, but not very serious with his studies, which I couldn't understand. He would always accuse me of studying too hard and not enjoying life.

My aunt and uncle were known as my adoptive parents and guardians, and my cousin as my brother. My uncle worked for the World Health Organization, a branch of the United Nations. The few students who knew I was from a village in Africa asked me so many questions about life in the jungle with all the animals in mud huts that I stopped telling people I was from the village. I would regretfully assume the identity of the son of a United Nations diplomat, like my cousin. I would use my cousin's stories as my own. Curious students would recommend that I watch movies that showed Africa as a backward, very primitive continent. That was the basis for their impressions and curiosity. To their defense, much of my lifestyle had been primitive, but not all of Africa is like that.

I was excelling at school. Initially I had some problems with understanding the teachers, but then compensated by studying very hard. Most of my classmates who couldn't understand my accent assumed I couldn't read well and offered to help me study. It was after our first set of tests that everything changed. Our first chemistry test was fifty multiple-choice questions, plus two bonus questions for an extra four points. Everyone was nervous. We checked into class for the one-hour test. To my amazement, many students were turning in their answer sheet twenty minutes into the test, thus announcing to the teacher that they were done. I was on question nineteen when the first student left the class. At forty-five minutes I was the only student left. Dr. Fletcher walked up to me and asked if I was doing okay. With sweat running down my face I nodded yes. He reassured me to take my time, that I still had fifteen minutes. I completed the test in one hour. It was my first multiple-choice test, so I wasn't sure how I did. One week later, Dr. Fletcher walked into the class with the test results. He announced the class average score was 70, with the 54 the lowest and 104 the highest. He walked to my desk, handed me my papers and said, "Good job! Keep it up." I had made the 104.

The news quickly spread. I was making similar grades, and with that came regular offers from several students in my class to tutor or study with them. My self-esteem was building. Other students would also show up at the soccer field to watch us play. The soccer team was made up mostly of international students. On the weekends, we would invite the American students to play with us. It was how I made friends with students from other countries.

With all the academic successes and the excitement of daily life, I was still constantly being reminded that at the end of the year I might not have the funding to continue my education. I finished that year with a 4.0 GPA and was inducted into the National Honor Society. I couldn't wait to tell my uncle, who typically called every week to check on us. When he finally called, I was in my cousin's room. They spoke for over thirty minutes, with my uncle giving my cousin details of his summer plans and vacations. My uncle had gotten his son tickets to visit friends and families around the US. My cousin then passed the phone to me. My uncle said he was proud of me but had some bad news: my parents could not come up with money to keep me at the university. He couldn't afford to help either. He had talked to family members in the US, but no one was either able or willing to help. However, there was one Cameroon family in Texas that was willing to host me for the summer and could help me find a cheaper community college there. The problem with that was I had to find my way to Texas and be able to pay my tuition myself. Without much else to say, my uncle apologized and ended the conversation.

I went to my room and, once again, cried all day long. What in the world was I going to do? All of the time and energy getting me here, only for me to run out of money in my first year. What about all my new friends? I was walking away from them with a good chance that I would never see or talk to them again. I would not even get the chance to say goodbye. After I had collected myself, I called Mrs. Hodges to tell her the news. She already knew and had been trying to see how she could help. The school was willing to give me a partial scholarship, but I needed a full scholarship to be able to stay. Because I was a soccer player, we even looked into the possibility of me joining the football team as a kicker, but they couldn't offer me a full scholarship either.

Eventually, nothing would pan out. So, my cousin's roommate had a friend from Arlington, Texas who had offered to take me and drop me off in Fort Worth with the Cameroonian family. And that is how I ended up in Texas. Just like that, I loaded my little suitcase with all my belongings and rode for six hours with a student I had never met before to get me to Texas.

Children washing clothes in a river in my village where we also bathed.
Small pond in the front is the drinking water.

My induction into the Phi Eta Sigma National Honors Society in 1995.

My mother's current (updated) kitchen and her fireplace. Notice the smoke-stained walls.

I celebrated Christmas with Aunt Sophie in Fort Worth. She was my host mother in Texas.

Without a car, I mostly had to walk everywhere.

CHAPTER 6

WELCOME TO TEXAS

MY HOST FAMILY IN Texas was one of my first miracles in the US. It was the same family that took us to the Chinese Buffet during our brief trip through Texas on our way to Arkansas. They had two young boys and the wife was pregnant with their third son. The father was from the same region of Cameroon as my family, but grew up in the bigger town of Muyuka. He told me that he offered to help because he knew of the many people that my parents had raised and helped. His name was Francis, so I called him Uncle Francis and his wife Aunty Sophie.

Uncle Francis worked as a nurse's aide while sponsoring his wife through nursing school at Texas Christian University. His aspiration was to be a pastor and build a church locally. He also hoped to build a hospital someday in Cameroon, as he was tired of all the suffering and death in the country. They shared their two-bedroom apartment in Fort Worth with me.

When I came, they moved the boys to sleep together on the bunk bed and I took the other bed. Fortunately, I was able to live with them rent-free. I applied and was accepted into a community college two miles from where we lived. As soon as I was permitted to work, Uncle Francis helped me find a job at the same nursing home where he worked. We had the same schedule, making it convenient to get back and forth to work. My first job was as a janitor. I cleaned up the rooms and cafeteria. Though my job did not involve patient care, I was always available to do whatever was needed, including transporting patients. The nurses and nurse aides loved my work ethic, and within a month, the director of nursing signed me up to get my nurse's aide certification. In no time, I was averaging seventy hours a week. With my certification, I got another job as a nursing aide within walking distance from the first job. I would come to work with Uncle Francis, and at the end of our shifts he would drop me off at the next job on his way home. Some days, especially during the holidays, I would work between the two jobs and go home only every other day. He would take me to work and only take me back home after his shift the next day. I would often take naps at the nursing home, off the clock. I ate my lunches at Albertson's, about a mile from the nursing homes. Uncle Francis' goal for me was to save enough money to get my own car so there was more flexibility between work and school.

I finally raised enough money to go buy my first car. Without any credit I could only pay cash, and where else could you get a great deal with cash other than at an auto auction—or so I thought. Uncle Francis had bought his previous cars at auction, and had a friend who was an auction dealer. I paid the auction dealer $100 to help me bid on a car. All I had was $2000. It didn't matter what car I got, as long as it ran and was within my budget. I also paid him $150 to drive the car from the auto auction to our apartment in Fort Worth. It was a Nissan Stanza, twelve years old with a manual transmission. Now I had a car, but I still needed to learn how to drive.

Around this time, Uncle Francis made a trip to Cameroon with his entire family. While they were gone, I paid a co-worker at the nursing home twenty dollars to take me to work and bring me home. When Uncle Francis returned, he was very busy but would teach me to drive whenever he could. One Monday, after working a double shift every day that weekend, I overslept and would have been late for class if I walked, and the heat was unbearable. So, against his advice, I took the keys to the car and drove to school by myself that day, for the first time. It actually took me longer than walking because I drove very slowly and stalled a lot because I didn't know how to drive with a clutch. But after a couple of weeks, I had the confidence to drive myself to the driver's license office to take the test. I passed on the first try, but I think that was because the nice lady did not want to get back into my hot stuffy car without air-conditioning.

My summers in North Texas were quite miserable, even for someone from Africa. In my village, I could run around and enjoy the breeze or take a dip in one of the many springs and rivers to cool off. Here, I was stuck in my car driving on highways for hours with no air-conditioning, with occasional stops on the side of the road to add water into my radiator, which frequently overheated. Yes, I drove around with a gallon of water in my car everywhere I went.

Now that I had my own car and a driver's license, the sky was the limit. For the next three years I was in the Dallas-Fort Worth area. I held at least two jobs at any given time and took a full-time course load at the community college and a local university. I stayed with Uncle Francis for a year and eventually got my own apartment. My year with his family reinforced my dedication to succeeding. He frequently reminded me that my father was the most hardworking and disciplined man he knew. He left a lasting impression on me to never forget where I came from and to embark on a field of study where I could impact my community back in Cameroon.

In May 1997, while studying biochemistry for pre-medicine, I was enrolled in one of the hardest classes I had ever taken. It was a higher-level chemistry class, called quantitative analysis. Prior to this I had been taking basic science classes and doing very well, but I knew this was going to be challenging, considering that I also had two jobs to maintain, and it was very overwhelming. I took my seat in the back of my class, as I planned to occasionally sneak out for work. Some days, I would fall asleep after working the night before, and my hope was that being in the back of the class would make it less noticeable. This really didn't matter as the class only had about fifteen students. During the first few days we had to pick lab partners. Kathleen (Kat) Cummings, whom I had known from another class, picked me.

Once the lab session started, we occasionally were asked to team up with the person closest to us. Sitting next to us was a team made up of an Asian girl and an Indian guy. The guy was very talkative, but the girl very shy and reserved. She did not like people playing around during class. Kat and I would become friends and study partners. We were taking two other classes together and so we did most of our homework together. She also shared another class with the Asian girl, and knew her well.

One day Kat invited all of us to have lunch together at the school cafeteria. It was an awkward lunch because I would speak to Kat, and Kat would speak directly to our Asian friend, who never said a word to me. Then we had our first test, on which I did very poorly. The class average was 70 percent and I got a 60. This was so out of the norm for me. I am not sure what happened, and I hoped there would be a retake or maybe the teacher would grade on a curve, but apparently someone in the class made a 96.

As usual, I had excuses for not doing well—two jobs, monthly bills, missing my family—but we all agreed the test had been difficult. We were jokingly suggesting that if someone scored a 96 percent on the test, that person had advanced access to the test or was having an affair with the teacher. Many students dropped out of the class, but I couldn't because I had already paid my tuition. I had no choice but to pass the class.

One day Kat couldn't make it to lunch, so I was alone with the Asian girl. She had a strange name that I couldn't pronounce, so I asked her to spell it for me—it was Kyu Mee, pronounced Q-me. I complained about the test and shared my conspiracy theories. She quietly listened, let me finish, then she went off on me.

Kyu Mee said I needed to take my studies seriously. She had seen me showing up late to class and then falling asleep. Then she told me she made the 96 percent. How embarrassing! She didn't understand why I had to work so much. She, too, had a full-time job and was paying for her tuition. Her family's business had gone bankrupt and she had withdrawn from Baylor University two years earlier, so now she was attending a public university. We were from completely different backgrounds but already had so much in common. I was raised Catholic and she Buddhist. After listening to each other's stories, we realized we could help each other with school.

We exchanged telephone numbers, and throughout the semester we would call each other to discuss assignments. She offered to take notes for me in class when I had to skip for work. Kat, Kyu Mee and I supported each other and all passed the class, remaining close friends. During this time I was going through incredible financial hardships and many times wanted to quit school, but they both pushed me to stay and did everything they could to see me through it.

Kyu Mee would help me find jobs that were less time-consuming. One was with a Korean family looking for a tutor to teach their high school daughter calculus. It paid twenty-five dollars an hour, more than three times what I was making at my other jobs. She passed on the job because she knew I needed it more. She would do this repeatedly, not just for me but for everyone she knew. She cared more about other people than she did herself.

While other students were concerned about what type of car they drove or going to a party, Kyu Mee stayed focused on her education. Her car was as bad as mine—she drove an Oldsmobile with busted windows and faded paint—but she never seemed to care. One of the attributes that impressed me most about Kyu Mee was that she never criticized, judged or put anyone else down. And she would admonish me or others if we did so in her presence. We would talk to each other almost daily. We became close friends, especially when Kat moved back to Dallas to live with her parents after her husband joined the military and was deployed.

My jobs as a nurse's aide placed me in a very close personal relationship with my patients and their families. I proudly took care of their activities of daily living. My unit secretary job was at a hospital, which allowed me to develop trusting relationships with nurses and doctors. I initiated all the phone calls to the doctors and transcribed their orders. My cardiac monitor technician job gave me a glimpse of being an important part of

the medical team. I was in charge of monitoring the patients'
heart rhythms, and reported any abnormalities to the nurse or
doctors. On top of this, I had jobs in several department stores
as a customer service representative. But with an average pay of
just six dollars an hour, it was extremely hard to keep up with my
rent and tuition.

I took every job that came my way. I was exposed to
individuals who took advantage of the system to claim disability
or worker's compensation. But all I wanted was a job that would
provide me with the resources to get to the next stage of my life.

One job was as a warehouse laborer for a factory in nearby
Arlington, Texas. I was the youngest in the warehouse, but
the pay was a whopping eight dollars an hour. We built and
packaged several pieces of equipment made of fiberglass. It was
hard labor, the warehouse had no air-conditioning, and after
work it was difficult to take a shower with fiberglass particles
embedded in my skin.

I kept working hard until one day, I was involved in an
accident. I was transporting a sheet of metal in the warehouse
when a tractor driver pulled in front of me. The metal rolled
over my forearm and made two deep cuts. I was afraid I would
be fired if I told anyone, so I went to the men's room, cleaned
it up and dressed it with paper towels and tied it with a piece
of cloth. I would dress it every day for a week and go to work in
long sleeves. A couple of my co-workers whom I told insisted
I report it, but I didn't. One night after work, it was so painful
that I drove to the nearest emergency room. I was diagnosed
with a wound infection and given antibiotics. The next day
while getting ready for work, I received a call by my supervisor
advising me not to come to work as they had decided to lay me
off. I asked why, and he said they were downsizing and would
call me when something came up. They never did.

With all the jobs I had been exposed to, I decided I wanted
to go into medicine. I visited and sought advice from the doctors
I worked with. My supervisors said that getting into medical
school with my grades and work-life experience would not be
a problem. One advisor even suggested that I apply to Harvard
University. So far, I had worked and paid my way through

undergraduate studies, but I could not do this in medical school. My advisors told me I would have to get a scholarship and financial aid. And so, we started calling all the medical schools in Texas to get advice and recommendations.

After sending my transcripts to several schools, I received a call from an advisor at Texas Tech University in Lubbock who informed me that with my grades I would easily qualify for a program that would guarantee me an entrance to their medical program. However, the program was only open to Texas Tech students. I would have to transfer and finish my undergraduate studies at Texas Tech. Moving away from friends and the only family I had known at the time should have been a tough decision, but it came easy for me due to the overwhelming financial and personal hardship, especially between 1997 to 2000. It was a struggle to keep up with my education while balancing other parts of my life.

In 2000, when I decided to load up all my belongings and move to West Texas, I was at the lowest point in my life. I was failing at almost every aspect of my life, including my faith. It was one of those times in life when I questioned whether God had forgotten about the plan He had for me. I often questioned whether I would have been better off staying in Cameroon, working on the farms that my father had labored to provide for me. As his first son, unless I did something incredibly displeasing to him, I would inherit most of his property per our tradition. I would certainly have three meals a day. Instead, he sent me to the US to study, work hard and come back and improve the situation in Cameroon. Because my father sold his farm for me, I had left my family worse off than if I had stayed and continued to farm the land to provide for them. I was willing to work, and I sure did while living in Texas. But year after year, I found myself stuck in the same place, living paycheck to paycheck, moving from one low-income apartment to the next, pleading with rental offices to give me a few more days. I couldn't tell my family how bad my situation was. There was nothing they could do.

I took the minimum hours of college coursework because I either couldn't afford more hours, or it conflicted with work. I knew at that rate, I would never be able to graduate from college and live up to my dreams and the dreams of my parents. I needed a miracle.

I spoke to a few friends about the move to Lubbock. I didn't tell many people because I didn't want anyone to change my mind. They had no idea how bad my situation was. Most people I spoke with highly discouraged the move. I was told that West Texas was a desert, it was very backward, and quite a few people told me that there were no black people in Lubbock and the people were racist. But at this point in my life, no amount of discouraging was going to keep me from moving on. I told myself that nothing could be worse than the situation I was currently in.

I had researched Lubbock, including searching for job openings in hospitals and whether they'd hire me during the summer before school started. I eventually talked to Mary Edwards, a nurse manager at Covenant Medical Center, a hospital in Lubbock that was very excited to receive my application. They had just put her in charge of a new department that would hire employees at higher pay rates with fewer benefits, to work on demand in different departments in the hospital. With my credentials, I would be guaranteed work every day. She created a new position for me called patient care technician III (PCT III), incorporating the three things I could do: hospital secretary, cardiac monitor technician and nurse's aide. Starting pay was eleven dollars an hour. I was sold.

I rented a U-Haul, packed all my things and was on my way to West Texas. That summer, I worked hard while waiting for school to start and to visit with a Texas Tech advisor. I was anxious. I had mapped out my future plans for medical school. When we finally met, he told me he had tried calling but my phone number was disconnected. He had bad news; he found out that I did not qualify for the Texas Tech medical school admission program. He was visibly devastated and apologized for the misunderstanding. I was equally disappointed, but understood that he couldn't help.

On top of that, I did not qualify for financial aid for several reasons, with one of them being that I hadn't registered with the US Selective Service System. Until the day I received the letter asking for proof of my registry, I had never heard of Selective

Service, which apparently requires all males to register at age eighteen, and is a prerequisite for applying for financial aid. But not knowing wasn't an excuse. I would eventually appeal and qualify, but at this time I was out. I talked to the nurses I worked with at Covenant Hospital who recommended nursing school. One of them gave me directions to the Texas Tech nursing school admissions office.

The next week, between work hours, I made phone calls to everyone I knew for advice or assistance. Nothing came through. The nurses at the hospital advised me to try gaining admission to nursing school at Texas Tech. That advice would change my life—by accident—and it was nothing short of a miracle.

One morning I took all my transcripts and drove to the building. The nursing admissions office was on the third floor, but I mistakenly got off at the second floor with the lady in the elevator with me. The building was massive and I easily got lost. I walked around, looking for any open doors, when I found myself in front of an office labeled Clinical Laboratory Sciences. I walked in, excused myself and asked for directions to the nursing program. Ms. Stephanie Cardenas politely gave me directions and wished me a good day. I started walking away, but then I turned around. I was curious and asked what kind of program Clinical Laboratory Science was. She explained to me that it was Medical Technology, the people who work in the hospital laboratories. I asked her what the requirements were to get into the program. She handed me a pamphlet and explained the requirements to me. I reached into my folder and showed her my transcripts, and told her if my meeting with the nursing admissions office didn't go well, I might come back to get more information about applying for the next year, as the program was already a week into the summer semester. She asked me where I was from and why I was in Lubbock. I told her my story and, little did I know, the program director, Dr. Lori Rice-Spearman, was next door listening in on our conversation. She walked into the room and asked to see my transcripts. She told me my grades were as good as the grades in her current class. Then she asked me a question that would change the course of my life. She asked, "If I were to admit you into the program, would you be able to start classes tomorrow?" I stared at her for a moment and told her I had no money for tuition. She said, "That is not what I asked you." She looked at me as if she wanted me to say yes. I said "Yes, ma'am." She asked Ms. Cardenas to give me an application form. I was to fill it out and bring it back to her at 9 a.m. the next day. I spent hours filling out the form, and totally forgot about my appointment with the nursing program. I worked from 7 p.m. to 7 a.m. that night, went to my apartment, cleaned up and went to Dr. Spearman's office promptly at 9 a.m. Ms. Cardenas took me to meet Ms. Carie Woodward at the admissions office where they had everything ready for me to sign. Next we went to the bursar's office where I signed a short-term tuition loan, to pay back in three installments throughout the semester. We went back to Ms. Cardenas's office and Dr. Spearman handed me a bag of textbooks and took me to my first class, which was already in session, and she introduced me to my new classmates. She had told the faculty members of the CLS program about me, and asked if anyone had extra textbooks to spare for me to use for my first semester. They had gathered most of my required books. The ones they didn't have I simply borrowed from the school library.

For the next two years I worked at nights and went to class during the day, and did extra work shifts on the weekends. I now had someone who believed in me, and I couldn't afford to let her down. I can say that between work and school I had no room for any distractions or leisure. Other than study groups with friends, I had nothing else going on in my life.

It was tough for me. There was no time for extracurricular activities. But after those two long, hard years, all my work paid off. I was able to graduate. Walking across that stage was one of the most incredible days of my life. I had received several academic and leadership awards and was picked by the faculty to represent the entire Health Sciences Center graduating class of 2002 as the flag bearer. I walked up to the stage to collect my diploma from Dr. Smith, the university chancellor, standing next to Dr. Lori Spearman, our program director. I was in tears, and so was Dr. Spearman. I reached out to shake Dr. Smith's hand, but instead he pulled me closer, gave me a hug and whispered to me that he knew all about my story and was proud of me. He said to keep shooting for the stars, and if I ever needed him to feel free to contact him. Then I gave Dr. Spearman one big hug. She was the one person in this room who truly knew my story and believed in me from the beginning. I had worked so hard to make her proud. I did not have a single family member at the graduation ceremony, but felt like family surrounded me. I had found my new home in Lubbock. After graduation, one of my classmate's parents invited me to lunch with their family. I went to work that night, where there was a party in honor of my graduation hosted by my co-workers. After passing my board exams I got a pay increase and continued working at Covenant hospital. However, everyone around me saw something in me and would not let me settle until I had reached my fullest potential. I worked as a medical technologist and enjoyed the job, but I missed the patient care aspect of my previous jobs. I also wanted to be in a profession that I felt would have the most impact in Cameroon.

In 2002, I graduated from Texas Tech Health Sciences Center, Clinical Laboratory Science program.

Jenny Bonner assists me as I prepare to lead the Texas Tech Health Sciences Center graduating class of 2002, as flag bearer.

My first car in Texas.

I received a leadership award for promoting diversity during a graduation event in 2002.

With Dr. Lori Rice-Spearman at a graduation event in 2017.

CHAPTER 7

MEDICAL TRAINING

WITH MEDICAL SCHOOL OUT of the question, I started looking toward other prospects. Then one day I made a casual visit to Texas Tech to visit Dr. Spearman. Interestingly, Ms. Cardenas, the woman who had sparked my initial curiosity, was no longer there. She had transferred to the Physician Assistant program department in Midland, Texas. Dr. Spearman told me I should consider the Physician Assistant program, too. I was familiar with the program, but was not quite sure how the role fit into the medical team. She went on to explain that to me, and discuss how I might be a good fit for such a position. Physician Assistants practice medicine in collaboration with physicians and are trained in the medical school model. As she pointed out, the benefits of the program were that it lasted 27 months, it was affordable, and had a great salary potential. For me, it was eye-opening. She thought it was perfect for my situation and urged me to look into it. So for months, I shadowed several Physician Assistants (PAs) and did my research on the profession. It passed all my basic checks, the two most important ones being that it would take me back to clinical patient care, and would advance my clinical expertise to improving the healthcare situation in my community at home in Cameroon. I applied to several Physician

Assistant programs across the country but hoped to get into the Texas Tech program located in Midland partly because, at this stage, I was tired of moving. I had already graduated from one of their programs and had many friends that I wanted to stay close to.

Texas Tech was also on my mind for another reason: my friend Kyu Mee wanted to go to graduate school and pursue a career in pharmaceutical research. She had been accepted into several schools, including Texas Tech University. I had been in Lubbock and was experienced with the people, climate and most importantly, the affordable tuition. So, I sold Texas Tech to her, not knowing at the time that this was to be the turning point in our relationship. After helping her move into her apartment, she asked where I attended church and said she would like to accompany me. I knew this would be interesting because I was Catholic and she was Buddhist. The first time we went to church together, she asked me several questions about the meaning of the different parts of the service. I bought her first Bible as a gift and we would spend a great deal of time studying it together. Finally, I got up the nerve to ask her out on a real date, all the while thinking, *She could have any guy, why in the world would she want to go out with me?*

With our busy work and school schedules, we could get back to helping each other in our aspirations. Kyu Mee would help me do my homework on Midland. We found out that the cost of living was very low: an average one-bedroom apartment cost $375. Midland had been an oil-rich town, but after the oil wells dried up in the '80s, the companies all packed up and left, leaving the town with more housing and infrastructure than they knew what to do with. More importantly, it was in West Texas and, at this stage in my life, close to my new home. My letter for an interview came really fast. I was excited but nervous.

The interview was supposed to be similar to that for medical school and they would want to know my level of maturity and motivation for wanting to become a PA. The day of my interview came. I walked into a large boardroom and was asked to sit at the end of this gigantic table. On the other end were the dean and two other members of the faculty. I knew the dean from my clinical lab science program, but was certain he had no idea who I was. Everyone was very serious. They asked me questions about my grades and educational background, especially since I had transcripts from four different schools. This was not typical of what they saw, and I did my best to explain to them my educational history. They asked me a series of questions, including challenges I had faced in my life and how I had overcome them. One particular question made me so emotional, I do not even remember how I answered it. Then they asked me why they should choose me over any other student. I think I was in tears by this time, and I don't remember that answer, either. The last question was about how I planned to improve my patients' lives by being a physician assistant. I believe I went into a rant about my life, my understanding of God's purpose for me and how I planned to change the world. I don't recall if any of my answers were religious, but at that point I did not care.

I was stopped in the middle of my explanation and informed that the interview was over, and they would contact me with their decision. It was very abrupt. I am not sure if I had given them the answers they were looking for. I thought, *Why did they stop the interview? Had I said too much? Did I get too religious? Did I say something wrong?* Walking out of the room, I saw Stephanie Cardenas and some other health sciences employees, my own cheerleaders, who were waiting to find out how it went. I told them I screwed it up. But a couple of days later, I received a call from the director of admissions informing me I had been accepted into the program. She informed me that I was one of the early decisions, and that I would be getting a formal letter in the mail. I was also granted the President's Scholarship. All I needed to do next was send a $50 fee to accept their offer and save my spot. Before she got off the phone, she told me everyone at the admissions office was very excited about me and hoped that I would cancel all my other upcoming interviews. As soon as I got off the phone, I wrote a check for $50 to secure my spot and drove to the health sciences center to make the payment before they changed their mind.

Knowing that I was accepted into the program, I was once again faced with challenges. My physician assistant training was unlike anything I had ever done before. I would have to quit my job in Lubbock and move 120 miles away to Midland for studies. That also meant being away from Kyu Mee and other close friends in Lubbock.

While all this was going on with me, the pharmaceutical industry was collapsing and Kyu Mee was worried about the job market. Her goal was to get a doctorate in biochemistry and work in the pharmaceutical research industry. She had already been awarded a patent for her research work at Texas Tech. So she decided to switch gears. She is one of the smartest people I have ever met, and so I convinced her to apply to medical school. She took the MCAT, but admitted to me that clinical medicine wasn't for her. She had never been exposed to direct patient care, while I had spent my entire life in the US exposed to every profession in the medical field. She thought pharmacy school would be a better fit. She passed the Pharmacy Technician Certification examination and took a job as a pharmacy technician at University Medical Center in Lubbock, while taking the prerequisite classes for pharmacy school. If accepted, she would have to move to Amarillo to attend the Texas Tech Pharmacy program. Despite being committed in our relationship, I knew the distance would be a challenge to us both. I feared that without me around, she would lose interest.

As I started PA school, I knew this was going to be a financial strain as well. The faculty all understood my financial situation. They were very helpful in finding scholarships that they thought I could remotely qualify for. I had received grants and scholarships from about six organizations, including the Texas Catholic Association, the American Academy of Physician Assistants (AAPA), and the Texas Tech University Health Sciences Center.

One faculty member who took an interest in me was Tammy Ream. She was part of my interview panel, so she was very familiar with my story. She supported and encouraged me. She even introduced me to her husband and kids. I quickly became fond of her.

At the end of the first month of school, the students were told we had to plan a class election to pick our class leaders. Students talked about the election, about people they thought would be a good leader, and so forth. I wasn't part of any of the conversations because I didn't see myself as a leader or ever having people skills. Then, one afternoon after classes, Mrs. Ream called me into her office. She started by asking me if I was running for any office. I told her I had no interest in a leadership position. She had heard about my work ethic from my medical technology program teachers in Lubbock. They apparently also told her that I got along with everyone in the class and was good at bringing people together, though I was not sure how they came up with that conclusion. In any case, she told me that they had had problems uniting some of their previous classes.

She thought I had something that the program needed—the ability to lead, listen and understand people. Then she asked if I was serious about everything I told them during my interview, to which I responded a resounding "Yes!" Then she asked how I planned to accomplish these things if I thought I couldn't even lead a class of thirty-five students. I told her I had been doing community services while in Lubbock and intended to continue in Midland. Then she told me that God wanted to use me as an instrument, not only to make a difference in the lives of the poor, but also to be a light to the people around me. She said many people had been placed in my life to keep me grounded in my mission. It was a refreshing change to have someone in a state institution talk about God's purpose for my life. I felt like I was talking to a spiritual leader.

Mrs. Ream went so far as to invite me to join her family on Sundays for church service. Then she talked to me about all the positions open for election, but strongly encouraged me to be the student representative for the Texas Academy of Physician Assistants (TAPA). It would involve organizing events at local, state and national levels. It also involved travel all over the US, but the Academy would cover my cost. At times I might be required to vote on issues that involved students. I would not only represent my school but all PA students in the state of Texas. She thought this would be a good means of getting me out of my shell, and it could help me develop my people skills. She said there would be some campaigning involved, but all I would have to do is make a presentation in front of my classmates. I was terrified of public speaking, but she said, "Just be you."

Election day came, and I found out I was running against a very popular and well-liked classmate. He was an athletic trainer prior to going into PA school, and was a very outgoing and equally intelligent individual. Everyone knew his name. I didn't think anyone knew mine—except the only other African-American in my class, Shelton. I had a three-minute speech prepared, and in my mind it wouldn't have bothered me if I had lost. My opponent spoke first, gave all his credentials and spoke of why he was the perfect candidate. It was such a good speech that even I would have voted for him. I should have gone first. It is so much harder to follow after someone gives a good speech. But there I was, standing in front of my classmates, giving a speech. After we were done and the votes were in, I guess Mrs. Ream was right. I was what the class needed because I won the election.

In no time the real work would start. On top of my very demanding course load, I had something going on all the time. Before every event I would visit Mrs. Ream, who at this time had become my mentor. I would start by organizing social activities to unite our class. A very close friend who lived in the same apartment complex helped me organize a pool party. We would have volleyball tournaments, Habitat for Humanity events, and food drives. One of the most exciting events was the Student Challenge Bowl, which was organized by the American Academy of Physician Assistants. It was a competitive elimination event, sort of like an academic *Jeopardy*. It started with all the PA programs competing at their individual state conferences. The winners would then compete at a regional conference and then advance to the national conference. My school had never participated before, but Mrs. Ream encouraged me to get my class involved. The school's offer to pay travel expenses enticed students to participate.

The state conference was in Dallas. We faced several schools such as University of Texas Southwestern, Baylor University, University of Texas Medical Branch Galveston and the University of North Texas. Our team consisted of two good friends, Leah Hall and Robert Baldree, and myself. I must admit, they were both better at the quick *Jeopardy*-style quiz than I was. We won, and a few months later we were in Austin competing for the regional tournament against the champions from eight other states. This time Leah couldn't make it, so another classmate, Trish Trevino, took her place. The school bought our flights and put us in a nice hotel. We were super excited to be in Austin. The brother-in-law of one of my teammates owned a bar on Austin's 6th Street. He took us to lunch at a fancy seafood restaurant overlooking Lake Austin that afternoon. He promised us that, if we won, he was going to host a party at his bar for us. Well, we won, and so the party was on. It was very exciting for everyone in our program, as we were the underdogs who entered the competition for the first time. We would represent our region comprising eight states at the national conference in Las Vegas. As a result, we were featured in the local news and the Texas Tech newsletter. Unfortunately, we lost in Las Vegas, but we had made leaps and bounds. We still celebrated like winners.

My position as student representative of TAPA also took me to Juarez, Mexico on a mission trip, a trip to the Texas state capitol where I met our local state representatives, a trip to Alexandria, Virginia, where I met the leaders of our national academy, and many more places. Most importantly, I visited the US Capitol in Washington, DC. In my first year of PA school, I travelled more than I had in all my previous years in the US.

I handed over my responsibilities in my final year of PA school to the incoming class, as my classmates were all getting ready for our clinical rotation. After the didactic part of our studies, we were each sent to one of five available sites for clinical rotations. People who were married or had children had priority. I was most interested in a place where it was cheap to live, and where I would get exposure to diseases common in Africa. So, I picked El Paso, Texas, which borders Mexico. With the high immigrant population there, I knew I would be exposed to diseases prevalent in Third World countries. It was the perfect fit for what I needed.

Everything was set until I received a call from Cameroon that my father was very sick and had to be taken to the hospital. Dad's blood sugars were running very high, and he was going in and out of consciousness. He also had a persistent nonhealing wound on his right great toe. He had been diagnosed with diabetes five years earlier and had been managing it with medications that were expensive.

While I was still in Lubbock I had talked to several doctors about Dad's case, and they had made recommendations as to his treatment. I would pass this information to my parents. Frequently the doctors would give me samples of medications to send to him. Based on the information I was getting and my basic knowledge, I knew he needed to be on insulin, but with no healthcare facility close to his home and no electricity to refrigerate his medications, this was impossible. As a student, I was not in a position to bring him to the US for treatment, and even if somehow I could manage that, Dad would have to go to El Paso, and I knew nobody there yet. To place myself in a position where I could pay for treatment for my father, I would have to go to Lubbock instead for my rotations. Knowing all the rotation sites were full, I went to Mrs. Ream to tell her about my situation. She visited with the program director and clinical coordinator who both agreed with her that it was next to impossible, unless I could figure out a way for the Lubbock facilities to take on an additional student.

Before Christmas break, I visited with all my classmates from Lubbock who I knew would be going home to spend the holidays with their families. Some of them had connections with the preceptor doctors at the different clinical rotation sites in Lubbock. I asked them to help me find a doctor willing to take an additional student for training. A friend's father was in charge of Internal Medicine at a large hospital in Lubbock. Another friend had been an emergency room nurse there for many years. Between the two of them campaigning for me, I was able to get clinical sites approved by the coordinators. So now I would be making plans to travel back to Lubbock and find a new apartment.

One of my classmates, Mike Reddell, approached me and invited me to stay with him and his family at their home in Lubbock during our year-and-a-half rotation. I wanted to make sure he understood I wasn't looking for a free place to stay, and so I thanked him and said I was very capable of paying for my own place and really didn't need help. He said he understood, but that he and his wife had talked and prayed about it and felt called to offer me a room at their home, rent-free. He gave me three reasons: He needed someone serious like me to study with and keep him focused, as we had already been study mates through our first year of the program. Secondly, he had a ten-year-old son who was very athletic and intelligent, but had never been exposed to someone from a different cultural background. Thirdly, he wanted to show his appreciation to me for helping him study pharmacology, which he had difficulties with.

Mike Reddell went into PA school after being a flight nurse for eighteen years. He was one of the students we all went to for help solving problems about clinical diagnoses and treatments. There was nothing Mike hadn't seen in the field. He was a tremendous resource for us all. However, he had been out of school for many years, unlike some of us "professional" students, so he was struggling to get back to the day-to-day didactic course load. He had a home in Lubbock and a temporary apartment in Midland. He would spend the weekends with his family in Lubbock, and then drive to Midland every Monday morning for the week. It was a huge sacrifice for him, and to this day I am not sure how he did it.

When I first met Mike, I had found him a bit intrusive. After one of our many pharmacology tests, Mike walked up and asked how I did. I wouldn't tell him my score, only that I did very well. Then he asked, "How well?" I remember Mike looking emotional. He explained that he was on the verge of failing the class, and needed someone who was doing well to help him study. He had given up his job of eighteen years to enter the PA program and couldn't fail. I told Mike that I had scored 100 percent on that test and would be more than happy to study with him. After that, we stayed close and continued to study together until graduation. If I was going to bring my father to the US for treatment, Mike wanted to make sure Dad had a place to stay. Mike's wife, Donna, was a wound-care nurse who too wanted to help. She gave me advice that I would pass on to Cameroon as to how to take care of my father's diabetic wound.

For every rotation I went through, my goal was to go above and beyond expectations. I knew that I still had some disadvantages, even though I now called Lubbock home and wanted desperately to get a job in the area after graduation. The Lubbock medical community was predominantly white, serving a predominantly white population. But I had fallen in love with the people and wanted to stay in the area, partly out of appreciation for what they had done for me. However, I wasn't sure if they would trust an African with an accent with their health. I did not know a single black PA, and knew of only three African American doctors in the area. One was a Nigerian cardiologist who had moved into town during my days as a nurse's aide. He was very good and had started a successful practice. But within six months he was gone. I never heard his side of the story, but people in the healthcare community said he was very arrogant with his staff, partners and hospital nurses. The patients complained about his bedside manner, and eventually the administration let him go. Keeping this in mind and remembering how my father always told me not to worry about the things I couldn't control, I worked very hard to prove to anyone who met me that I was just as good as or even better than any other PA out there.

I realized that first I would have to work extra hard to prove this to the doctors who were training me during my rotations. On some rotations, I was with medical students and residents. During a typical grand rounds, we had the attending physician leading the team down the halls, and next to them were the senior residents, then the interns, then the medical students. I was usually at the back of the crowd. If the attending physician looked in my direction when posing questions, and I answered correctly, I would be standing next to him or her by the end of the rotation. I wasn't the smartest or most naturally gifted, but I always strived to be the hardest working.

If questions were asked that nobody knew how to answer, I would spend hours at the end of the day looking up the answers, because I knew these questions would be asked again. Now that I didn't have a night shift job to go to, I stayed up most nights reading up about potential procedures for the following day. This was after doing my own rounds, reviewing patients' records and familiarizing myself with why they were admitted to the hospital and their working diagnoses. I would work out a treatment plan and potential complications. By morning rounds, I knew everything there was to know about our patients. This would prove to pay huge dividends as I completed my training and got ready for the job hunt.

Six months prior to graduation, while most of my classmates were worried about the job market, I already had five job offers. One offer was to work in a rural emergency room outside of Lubbock. There was a businessman who wanted to open an occupational medicine facility in Lubbock and have me run it. There was an offer to work in a very busy emergency room in Lubbock. One of the most exciting offers was from a very busy Internal Medicine doctor who was well-respected in the community, and I had a wonderful experience during my clinical rotation with him. He was very intelligent and worked very hard. I thought he never went to sleep. He had multiple roles in the community, including being the main internal medicine physician for a four-hundred-plus-bed hospital. He was the medical director and the chief physician for several nursing homes throughout West Texas and Eastern New Mexico. He had several excellent Advanced Practice Providers working for him. He also had a private plane to travel to the other facilities. I was fortunate enough to accompany him on many trips.

This prospective employer had a doctorate in biochemistry and had done groundbreaking research in diabetes. He represented and spoke for several pharmaceutical companies. Even with all this, he still knew the names of his patients and their medical problems. He approached me and told me he wanted me to help manage his hospital patients in Lubbock. I was flattered. The salary was very lucrative, for a kid fresh out of training. But I had a lot to think about. This was a very busy practice taking care of some of the sickest patients in the region. As his midlevel provider, I would encounter very high expectations from the medical staff. I would get the first call from the hospital for any issues, and then try to get in touch with the doctor if there was something I couldn't handle. If I took this job with its large workload, would I be able to travel to Africa?

Amazingly, for every week that went by without a commitment from me, my compensation offer package improved. First, it was an increase in my base pay, and then commission based on my productivity. Then the offer got even more interesting. The doctor had a beautiful red BMW 330 convertible that he kept in one of the airports outside of town, and only drove when going to see out-of-town patients. I had driven the car with him on multiple occasions during my clinical rotation. He offered it to me, and all I had to do was pick up the payments. He also owned a residential construction company and built houses and condominiums. I was offered one of his condos, with six months rent-free, as a bonus. Then the pot was sweetened even more. One morning during rounds, he told me that if I took the job, he would love to train me to become a pilot, so I could fly to surrounding towns to see patients. You would have expected me to be excited, but I was terrified. I had flown with him on several occasions in his little plane. Though he was an excellent pilot, I was terrified every time we flew. Had my learning to fly become a condition of employment?

I finally turned to my friend and roommate, Mike, who advised me to pray about it. I decided to visit our next-door neighbor who was a pastor. After praying with me and hearing about my goals in life, the pastor asked me how I could accomplish all these things and still keep up with the schedule this job was offering. Then he asked me how I felt about the job. I told him how much I enjoyed working with the doctor and respected him, but all of the lavish benefits and pay just didn't sit well with me. I told the pastor I had seen poverty beyond belief and needed money, but that I was not willing to relinquish my dreams for this job. The pastor told me to pick up the phone and turn down the job offer.

I worried that turning down the job offer from one of my preceptors might tarnish my other job prospects in Lubbock: the man I had just rejected was one of the most influential and recognizable names in the Lubbock community. Thankfully, he was very supportive of my decision and offered to help if I ever needed him. So I still didn't have a job.

As fate would have it, on my last rotation in the emergency room, I worked with several doctors including Dr. Haning, a very humble, well-loved and beautiful person that everyone wanted to be around. She had a way of making every patient and staff member feel that during your time with her, nothing else existed in her world but you. I had assisted her on several procedures and had a few conversations with her about my life. Then one day, she asked me if I already had a job lined up. She was surprised when I said I didn't, that I had turned down every offer. She said she had a job for me. Her daughter was married to an orthopedic spine surgeon in Tyler, East Texas. She wasn't sure if he was looking for a PA, but she felt that he was busy enough that he needed help so he could spend more time with his family. I could tell she had a special relationship with her son-in-law and wanted what was best for him and his family. Asking me to be part of that world was a huge compliment.

Tyler was much closer to Fort Worth, where I had Uncle Francis, and he and his wife would help care for my dad if he needed to come to the US for medical treatment. Within weeks, I was in Tyler for an interview and instantly fell in love with Dr. Haning's family. For a much lower pay than the internal medicine job offer, I took the job, and after graduation I packed up and once again moved back to East Texas. Compared to the wide-open plains of West Texas, East Texas was beautiful. It reminded me of Cameroon, with the tall trees, the fresh smell of roses everywhere, and many hills and lakes. I was enjoying my job and the people were wonderful—but it wasn't West Texas. It was a little harder to assimilate into the medical community. The impression I got was that doctors and administrators whose influence spanned generations controlled the medical community. They were not interested in newcomers or new ideas. My boss faced the same challenges, but he was white, so I knew it wasn't about race.

For the year that I was in Tyler, I did not succeed in making any long-lasting friendships outside of my boss, his family and the office staff, but it wasn't for lack of trying. I did several community outreach activities and got involved in the soccer league. At the same time, I missed Kyu Mee, who was now attending the Texas Tech School of Pharmacy in Amarillo. This separation was a major strain on our relationship. Also, she had told me that after pharmacy school she would want to move back to the Dallas area, to be close to her family: without me in Lubbock, she saw no reason to move back there. Additionally, my father had made it clear that he would not be coming to the US, as the journey would be too much for him, plus his condition was stable enough now with the help of his diabetes doctors in Cameroon.

One Friday afternoon in March 2006, after a busy day of work, I was sitting in my apartment watching *Seinfeld* while getting ready for a soccer game. My phone rang and I noticed it was a Lubbock area code, where I still had many friends. The guy on the line introduced himself as Dr. Richard George. He told me he had heard a lot about me and asked me if I was happy with my job. I told him I was. He asked me if I would consider moving back to Lubbock. I told him yes, because of my friends and girlfriend, but only after I had fulfilled my two-year contract. I could tell he was very distracted because he was watching his kids play soccer. He offered to buy me a plane ticket to Lubbock, to come visit and see what he had to offer. I agreed. I immediately got off the phone, called my girlfriend Kyu Mee and told her I had been offered a free ticket to come see her. I told her it was for a job, but I was sure I would not be taking it. She cautioned me not to accept the free flight offer if I would not be taking the job. I got off the phone and went to my soccer game knowing that, when Dr. George called back, I would be turning down the offer. I just didn't want to consider moving again.

He called back at 9:30 p.m. the same day and asked what my plans were for the weekend. I said I had no big plans for Saturday, but I had our soccer league championship game on Sunday. He offered to fly me to Lubbock on Saturday and promised to get me back to Tyler before the game on Sunday.

Knowing how expensive it would be to book a flight within such short notice, I told him not to waste his money as I was very happy in Tyler and most likely would not take his job offer. He insisted, and said he would call me early Saturday morning with the details of the flight. I accepted. As soon as I got off the phone, I started calling friends in Lubbock to find out about Dr. Richard George. He had gone to UT Austin for undergraduate school, to Baylor for medical school and MD Anderson for fellowship. He was board certified in pediatric neurosurgery and also treated adult neurosurgical and spine disorders. He had been in practice in Lubbock for twenty years and was the busiest neurosurgeon in West Texas, if not all of Texas. He was a founding member of the premier neurosurgical group in Lubbock. Patients came to see him from all over West Texas, Eastern New Mexico and even parts of Oklahoma. His medical group was made up of six neurosurgeons and six physician assistants. His last PA had gotten tired of the workload and left.

He called the next morning and again, I said I wouldn't be taking the position, but he insisted on sending his plane. I thought God must be testing me again. By one o'clock, I had my little bag packed with my only suit, the same suit I wore to my PA school interview and the most expensive thing I owned. Yes, it was more expensive than my car. I showed up at the private lounge at the Tyler airport and the attendant checked to make sure I was Sixtus Atabong. He then offered me coffee or anything else I would like to drink, and told me my plane would arrive in about thirty minutes. I was thinking, *I could get used to this*. I wished my dad could see this. He would see that, finally, all the hard work was paying off. He would be impressed by the treatment I was receiving.

A Cessna 182 airplane approached the runway. It was much smaller than the one owned by the internal medicine doctor. Then came the pilot, who I initially thought looked like a kid: *This could not be my pilot*. He walked up to me with a big smile and asked if I was Sixtus. He introduced himself as Myron, my pilot. By this time my heart was pounding. I couldn't hold back any longer, so I asked his age. He said twenty-three, and that I need not be worried; he was very experienced. *Experienced at twenty-three? When did he go to college?* I must be out of my mind getting on this plane with someone who was so much younger than me. But it was too late, as he already had my bag in his hand and was walking toward the plane. After a bumpy ascent, the plane leveled off and we cruised all the way to Lubbock. Sitting that close to Myron as he piloted the plane, I appreciated and was very impressed with his landing. I apologized for doubting him and told him I was looking forward to the return flight.

My visit to Lubbock went very well. Dr. George gave me a tour of the hospital and clinic and introduced me to the other partners and PA's in the group. I even ran into several nurses I already knew. He took me to his home and introduced me to his wife and kids. We had our formal interview in his living room with his wife present. Finally, he asked me where I saw myself in five years. Needless to say, I gave him the same pitch as from my PA school interview. Then he said he had always wanted to get involved in medical missions to underserved areas, but he was either too busy or couldn't figure out the right one to get involved in. He said he could feel my passion for missions and would do everything he could to help, but would also give me enough time off to travel to my home country and start whatever mission I felt was needed there. The group also offered to buy me out of my job contract in Tyler. It would take a few weeks to iron out the details, but eventually I realized I could not pass up this opportunity to go back home to Lubbock.

I accepted the job offer, a decision that would put me squarely back on track to fulfill my lifelong mission of returning to my home country and make a positive contribution to the healthcare disparity of my community. And joining me on this journey would be the beautiful Asian woman who helped me survive undergraduate school, and my new boss who would soon become my mentor. The road would be extremely difficult, but purposeful. Having Kyu Mee and the support of Dr. George along this journey would make all the difference in the world.

I worked with Dr. Shawn Conard during my clinical rotation in Muleshoe, Texas.

In 2005, I graduated from Texas Tech with a Master of Science in Physician Assistant Studies degree.

Graduation day at Texas Tech in 2005.

During my physician assistant training, I helped with a Habitat for Humanity event.

Mrs. Tammy Ream, RIP.

Ed Maxwell was my PA Program Director at Texas Tech.

I consider Mike and Donna Reddell to be part of my American family.
I lived with them during my PA clinical rotation.

Robert Baldree and Trish Trevino and me, after winning the
Student Challenge Bowl competition in Austin, Texas.

CHAPTER 8

FIRST TRIP
BACK HOME

WHEN SOMETHING FAVORABLE HAPPENS to us, we say we are blessed. We think of it as a gift from God, or a favor from someone. Rarely do we ask ourselves, *What did I do to deserve such a favor or how can I pay it forward?* I realized that my entire life had been built upon one gift after another—some from people I knew and some from others that I did not know. Some I would have the opportunity to repay; others I would never meet again, at least not in this lifetime.

I had pushed myself extremely hard to prove that these acts of kindness never went in vain. From the sacrifices made by my family on my behalf, to the people who have helped me along the way, I owed it to them to do my part to help others along their own paths. As my father would put it, "Our purpose on earth is to serve others as others have served us." Even as a student, I was thinking of how I could serve others. But first I had to go back and check on my family. I always wondered how my family in Cameroon survived without me. They too wanted to know how I had survived without them. I was especially anxious about seeing my ailing father.

While I was in PA school in Midland, Kyu Mee was in Lubbock working on her graduate studies in biochemistry. She had become one of my best friends, a friend I could talk to about everything I was going through. She knew all about my family and our struggles. She also understood that one of the reasons I hadn't gone back to Africa was because I had not been able save enough money to afford the $2,000 airfare. Knowing how badly I wanted to go home, she surprised me with the plane ticket to Cameroon to visit my family for the first time since I had left them in 1995.

During the Christmas break of my first year of Physician Assistant training, I was able to go back home for the first time in almost a decade. I received a welcome ceremony in my village fit for a king. There were celebrations by the women's association of the village, and youth dances by the kids and lots of food and drinks to go around. We talked about my life in America. I was certainly overjoyed to see my mother, my brother, my sisters, my father and my childhood friends. Through all the celebrations and catching up, I couldn't help but notice how everyone had aged in my absence. The hard manual labor had taken its toll. My father's health had deteriorated due to uncontrolled diabetes, and it was quite visible. One of my very close childhood friends had died. He was the son of my mother's best friend. He had been like a little brother and had looked up to me. Michael died at age twenty-five soon after complaining of a headache and fever. In the US, healthy people don't die from routine fevers or headaches. Images of poor rural life came rushing back with this news. I had seen my village people die some of the most senseless deaths, and my parents could do very little to shield me from it. Sickness was an everyday event. It seemed someone around me was always sick. By the age of eleven I had witnessed multiple deaths, three of which I could still remember quite vividly.

My village of Munyenge was very remote, but there were other villages on the old mountain road that the timber truck drivers had created. The closest bigger town was Muyuka, and everyone going to Muyuka from the farther, more remote, villages would have to trek or drive through my village. Cars were rare. If you had to go to Muyuka, the few trucks would leave from the motor park at the center of the village in the morning, and return in the evening. The distance was only about sixteen miles, but the terrain was quite treacherous. If you missed the early morning transportation trucks, you would have to wait until the next day.

When I was about nine, attending church on Sunday morning, a couple of villagers came and got my dad. There was a pregnant woman who was sick and had been brought to our village in the hopes of catching a truck that would take her to the closest hospital in Ekona, a town close to Muyuka. At that time, my dad's small farm truck had some mechanical issues, and there were no other vehicles available to transport her out of the village. My father took me with him to the village center, which at this time was crowded with after-church goers. The woman was lying down in a wheelbarrow padded with leaves and tree branches. Her husband and the family were drenched in sweat from transporting her from their town of Bakundu Banga, another ten-plus miles away. As soon as we showed up, she started convulsing. I witnessed my dad supporting the woman's head and barking orders. People were bringing in water, different herbs to rub on her legs, belly and chest. Nothing worked. This went on for about forty-five minutes. Then I saw the woman take her last breath. In the commotion, I don't think my dad even realized I was there. There were several other kids watching. After she died, the family burst into loud cries. I heard the husband saying, "Why, God, why?" over and over. The villagers came out to console them and help them load the woman's body back into the wheelbarrow for a long trek back to their village.

There was the popular soccer player in the village who died of tetanus. He injured himself during a major game that I was watching. He was well known as one of the toughest soccer players, as he would play the game without shoes. This was not uncommon, as most of us couldn't afford soccer shoes. If we did have shoes, they were rubber-covered shoes called Dschang Shoes, which offered no protection for your feet. The boy playing barefooted hit his large toe on a rock. The injury was so severe that he was taken out of the game. A few days later, his family brought him to our house for treatment.

A man who owned a pharmacy in Muyuka came to my village and rented one room in a building that my dad used as a store and a small bar. The pharmacy quickly became the village clinic. We called the owner "Dr. Apollo." The soccer player's family brought him in with a high fever and seizures. From my front porch I could see and hear my dad and several other villagers trying to open his mouth to give him the medications that the pharmacist had prescribed, but to no avail. My mother, hearing what was happening, came and told us to go inside. We could still hear the sound of struggle which typically ended with loud sorrowful screams. My dad would later explain to me that Dr. Apollo told the family that the boy had tetanus and there was nothing that could be done. There were no tetanus vaccines in the village. He was only fifteen.

The most impactful case was my own cousin, Brother Lawrence. He was the eldest son of one of my dad's brothers. I called him brother because he grew up with us. My dad's two brothers lived in a two-bedroom house behind ours that my father had built for them. Their kids lived in the same house with us.

As with many of my family members who lived with us, I didn't know who was my biological sibling and who wasn't. I thought we all had the same parents. When Lawrence got older, he moved out to live on his own. One day my parents were told that he had gotten very sick. After many attempts with traditional medical remedies, my father decided to put some money together and get him to a hospital. For a month, they took Lawrence from one hospital in the town of Buea to another in Limbe, and then to Douala. Finally, they brought him back home because the doctors said they couldn't find what was wrong. One traditional doctor told my parents that he was poisoned. When he came back home, my parents fixed a room behind our house so they could care for him there. Every day after my mom would cook, it was my job to take his food to him. My mom and his stepmother took turns bathing him and cleaning him. In the mornings, after Mom would make his breakfast, I would clean his room and report back to Mom that he was doing okay. Since no one knew what was making him sick, the villagers mostly stayed away. This went on for about two months. At this stage, he had lost so much weight that he couldn't stand or even get out of bed. His face was barely recognizable. None of his clothes still fit him. Our family was just waiting for him to die.

One morning, I went to take him breakfast and couldn't wake him up. I ran home to tell my mother who immediately got my dad and other family members. All I remember after that was the funeral procession to his grave. The kids were not allowed to observe the burial process. It was after this event that my father started talking to me about studying hard to be a doctor someday so that I could open a hospital in my village.

On this first visit home from the US, I was taken to what I was told was a new medical clinic in the village. It was staffed by a doctor with no formal training, a healer. The healer proudly talked to me about his medical practices, which mostly consisted of the use of herbs to treat everything from fever to wounds and headaches. As kids, we thought the traditional healers competed to see who could come up with the most bitter or pungent concoctions. Back then, the popular belief was that if a treatment wasn't painful or unpleasant, it most likely wasn't good. An example was using hot water to scrub wounds until they bled and then cover them with concoctions. The most gruesome treatment I experienced was used to prevent tetanus after a nail puncture. It involved putting a knife or machete into a fire until it became red hot, then putting drops of cooking oil on it which were immediately dripped into the puncture wound to kill the tetanus bacteria. Then there was the treatment for fractures. First, those who subscribed to traditional medicine believed that only twins could treat fractures. That was pretty much the only qualification you needed. Older twins start teaching the younger twins in the village how to treat fractures at a very young age. The treatment for a fracture was to massage the fracture site and then blindly align the bone and use bamboo sticks to wrap around the limb as a brace. It was a painful process.

Coming back to Cameroon after many years in the US, I better understood what my father was talking about. After my stay in the village, I traveled to my ancestral village of Fontem to visit my other family members. I also wanted desperately to go back to Seat of Wisdom to thank Principal Jane Dube who had taken a chance on me. She had passed away in 2001 from a car accident on the road to Fontem, and there was a monument in her honor that I wanted to visit. She was one of several who had died in Fontem while serving the people of the community. As a boy, when I had transferred to Seat of Wisdom, Fontem, I experienced what a group of people were doing to save a community that was close to extinction from diseases. It was called the Focolare Movement and they founded my secondary school in Fontem. Miss Jane was a volunteer with this organization who moved from England to Fontem.

It was well documented that the infant mortality in Fontem, prior to the arrival of the Focolare Movement, was over 90 percent. The chiefs had run out of answers from the traditional healers. At some point, it was discovered that the people were dying from sleeping sickness, a disease transmitted by the TseTse fly. These flies were transmitting the *Trypanosoma* parasite. Once in the human body, this parasite caused high fevers, headaches and extreme fatigue, and if not treated led to death. It was a disease that, if diagnosed, was easily treatable. However, the chiefs didn't know this at this time. Desperate for answers, the chiefs turned to the Catholic Church. They appealed to the local bishop for prayers and assistance. In 1962, the bishop was visiting Vatican City and met with Chiara Lubich, the founder of the Focolare Movement, and he shared the story of the Bangwa people. Because of that, in 1965, the first group of nurses and doctors from the Focolare arrived in Fontem and opened the first medical clinic. From this clinic came the Mary Health of Africa hospital, which is still operating today as the only major hospital in the area. A few years later, in coordination with and upon request by the chiefs, Seat of Wisdom College, Fontem was founded. Fortunately for me, I very rarely used the hospital as a student there; I didn't get sick once.

The volunteers of the Focolare become part of the Fontem community. They left their homes in Europe, Asia, the Americas and other parts of Africa. Some of the missionaries lost their lives from diseases they contracted in Fontem, but that never deterred the group. Chiara Lubich once said, "In life we do many things, say many things, but the voice of suffering offered out of love, which is perhaps unheard by and unknown to others, is the loudest cry that can penetrate Heaven." I felt that love every day of my four years at Seat of Wisdom.

Our teachers at Seat of Wisdom College taught us with love, the nurses and doctors at Mary Health of Africa treated us with love, even the principal of the school disciplined us with love. As kids, we may not have appreciated it. On my first visit back to Cameroon I certainly wanted to stop by and tell them how much I appreciated them now.

Over the years, Seat of Wisdom had expanded from a secondary school to include high school. I was honored to be one of thousands of former students who went back once again to the school in 2016 to celebrate and lay the foundation for a university on the campus. We, the beneficiaries of their love, are scattered all over the world. We are doing our part to extend their compassion to many others whom they couldn't reach. We are all living testimonies of the love that Chiara Lubich and her organization extended to us.

Through my years at Seat of Wisdom, I witnessed people showing compassion through mercy, love, and service. We were called to do more than praying. We were asked to reach out and extend the healing hand of Christ, especially to those who are suffering from physical and spiritual pain. This organization not only healed the sick in this community, it invested in the community's future by creating an institution to educate the children to be healthier and live longer. By doing this, they planted the seed of sustainability as those children are today the teachers, doctors, priests, pastors, and leaders in this community and around the world. I have seen what suffering does to a society and I have also seen what compassion can do.

As a recipient of what I consider one of the best examples of sustainable charity, my decision to embark on what we today call Purpose Medical Mission was not a difficult one. The people who would become the core of this organization would become like family to me. They would travel with me to many countries, leaving their families behind, to answer the call to serve. In addition to individual support, they would grow our charitable web, drawing together churches of different denominations, businesses all across West Texas, local banks, and even our two major universities, Texas Tech University and Lubbock Christian University. Our board would become a family of friends from all walks of life, all of whom understand the importance of being good stewards of people's generous gifts and God's unconditional love for the people we serve.

During my first trip back home, I visited my maternal grandparents' grave site in Fontem.

A Welcome Dance was performed by the women's group of
my village for my first trip back home.

I was happy to see my parents when I went home for the first time after 10 years.

The youth association celebrated my first trip home after almost ten years.

Two of my sisters, after our decade of separation.

Tribute to Miss Jane Mary Dube, Seat of Wisdom College principal.

I visited Mr. Nelson, Seat of Wisdom College principal.

At the Welcome Ceremony, I thanked everyone for their kindness.

Welcoming dance performed by the youth group of Munyenge.

CHAPTER 9

THE BIG PLAN

KYU MEE HAD BEEN very receptive to converting to Christianity, knowing that I would want to raise my children as Christians. She had taken a class for adult Catholics before baptism. In May 2007, she became a Christian, and a year later would agree to be my wife.

I was terrified to tell my parents about her. They had heard about her as a "friend" I cared about a lot, but we never discussed the idea of marrying someone from a different race. An uncle had already said "no" and advised me not to even think about telling my parents. As a distraction, my uncles and aunts would start introducing me to every African girl they knew. But for me, there was no other person I could see spending the rest of my life with. Kyu Mee and I had seen each other through the lowest points of our lives. She loved and believed in me when I was a student with nothing to my name. But I had to wait for courage to ask Dad. I wanted my father's admiration and blessing, and a woman to share my life with. When I finally asked my dad for his blessing to marry Kyu Mee, he laughed and told me he already knew my intentions and had been telling everyone to leave me alone. He said I had been living by myself without his guidance for over ten years and it was not his place to stop me. His only request was that I bring her to visit the family in Africa.

My relationship with Kyu Mee would also grow with our shared commitment to impact positive change in our circle of influence. For eleven years we both endured extraordinary hardships in our personal lives. We soon realized that, despite our different backgrounds and upbringings, the one thing we had most in common was how we approached adversities. We both believed that our individual struggles brought us closer to each other. I needed her more than ever to be by my side for this next chapter of my life. On December 29, 2007, I asked for her hand in marriage and she said yes. Exactly one year later, we became husband and wife. Ironically, it is Kyu Mee who holds me accountable today for following my father's teachings to be a better husband, parent and caretaker to our two sons, Zigo and Zi Chan.

I was by now a medical practitioner working for one of the busiest neurosurgery practices in Texas. I had only been on two mission trips—both as a PA student. First was the short trip to Juarez, Mexico with a group sponsored by the First Baptist Church in El Paso. There were doctors, dentists, nurse practitioners and students on this trip. The mission went extremely well. I couldn't do much more than assist the nurse practitioner with triaging patients. One patient was a seven-year-old girl. Her mother brought her in with an acute asthma attack. The nurse practitioner asked the mother how she usually treated her daughter and she said she used a traditional remedy, which sometimes worked and sometimes did not. The child was put in a room at the local Baptist church and we treated her with inhalers. She was doing great several hours later and was discharged. They were given the remaining tube of inhalers before they left. The mother thanked us and asked God to bless us.

On the way back home, everyone in the bus was feeling pretty good about what we had accomplished. We saw more than 200 patients, diagnosed and treated many, but some we couldn't help. I sat in the back because I wanted a quiet spot. I was quietly sobbing, thinking of what I had seen, and knowing the same problems were occurring in my village back in Cameroon with no one to take care of them. What saddened me the most was that I saw myself in that sick child we treated. As a child,

I was always sick with malaria, typhoid, chickenpox and every childhood disease you can think of. My parents had no idea what to do with me. They exhausted all traditional remedies for me and my sisters. I saw my mother cry frequently and ask God that if a child was a blessing, then why He would allow me to suffer so much. I once had abdominal pain so severe I would tie my belly really tight with a piece of cloth. It sometimes helped to simply create pain somewhere else, to distract me. One day my mom actually prayed for God to take me instead of allowing me to suffer.

I decided I had to do something to alleviate the pain and suffering in my village like we had done in Mexico. I started planning my mission to Cameroon, but I couldn't stop thinking of this little girl. What would happen when she ran out of medicine and returned to the makeshift hospital with her next asthma attack? We had left nothing behind to help them take care of themselves. What about all the patients we diagnosed with chronic illnesses such as hypertension or diabetes? We brought no medicines. We did give them a prescription to get their drugs from the local pharmacy. But could they afford it? How would we know what medicines worked best for them? How could we make sure that they were healthier in the future? Who would follow up to make sure that the remedies worked? I had more questions than answers. At least I had some clarity on how I wanted to approach a medical mission in my village. I wanted to replicate what the Focolare movement did in Fontem. If I was going to do anything, it was going to include the community and it was going to be sustainable. The first thing I had to figure out was how to help the people take care of themselves.

Four years after this trip to Mexico, I still couldn't get that little girl with asthma out of my head. Every year I wondered what became of her. With my very busy schedule, I had a plan mapped out—a five-year plan. I would save some money, go to my village, get the farmers to provide me with some land and build a clinic there. If I could erect a building, and get basic supplies such as blood pressure cuffs, blood sugar machines and wound care supplies, I could certainly convince a nurse from the city to come to the village and help me take care of the farmers. I had already sent my father to visit a chief who was very excited about the plan and he offered to do anything to help. The goal was to assist in the diagnoses and management of chronic medical illnesses such as hypertension, diabetes and common farming accidents. If my father had been diagnosed earlier and received some education about diabetes, perhaps his blood sugars would have stayed under control.

While saving money for the medical mission project, I was also trying to convince my father to slow down. The tedious manual labor of farming was detrimental. I offered to send my parents a monthly stipend to offset reduced farm income, but my seventy-year-old father refused. I was worried about accidents or him going into a diabetic coma while in the fields. He still insisted on climbing cocoa trees to trim or harvest the crops, or carrying the crops on his head from the farm to the house. And he was already having problems with arthritis, experiencing frequent joint and neck pain.

I decided to buy him a used farm truck from Japan and ship it to him. When I called the delivery driver I was shocked to hear that my father had been taken to the state hospital in a nearby city. He had a wound from a farming accident and my mother had been taking care of it at home for months. Dad had forbidden them from telling me for fear I would worry. The wound had gotten infected and involved his entire right leg. I was indeed very worried knowing he had uncontrolled diabetes, which could potentially make the wound fatal. I finally got ahold of his treating physician on the phone. He confirmed my fears; Dad had gangrene of his right foot with infection spread up to the right knee. His only chance of survival was amputation above the knee and use of intravenous antibiotics. I was devastated. This was a man who had worked so hard all his life, who had helped many people, had sacrificed for his family, and was going to be handicapped in a country without infrastructure or accessible transportation for amputees.

The truck that I purchased for him had been delivered to his house in Munyenge, but he would never be able to drive it. After the amputation, even if I got him a wheelchair, he would not be able to go anywhere except from his bedroom to the living room.

The house was not conducive for a wheelchair, nor the outside landscape of volcanic rocks with hills and trees everywhere. After the doctor told my father the news, Dad asked to speak to me. He begged me to convince my mother to let him die in peace. He refused the surgery and said he would rather be dead than have to depend on other people to clean him up or help him with daily activities. He had been independent all his life and would never impose such a hardship on anybody.

The local doctor didn't know what to do. He didn't have time to sit down and try to convince my dad, because he was the only government trauma surgeon in the state. He told me one of his biggest challenges was lack of basic supplies he could use to save his patients. Each patient going for surgery would be responsible for buying sutures, IV antibiotics, pain medications and all the fees prior to surgery. Medical supplies were available at local pharmacies, but they were often fake or very low-quality products imported from surrounding countries.

Getting my father to the US was not an option as he was too sick to travel. I decided I would rally the siblings to convince our father to have the surgery. He eventually agreed, and the surgery was performed at a hospital in Buea. The surgeon called with details; he had used Ketamine, an anesthetic agent used in the US mostly by veterinarians to put animals to sleep. He did not have a drill so he used a handsaw to remove my father's leg. The surgery took longer than he had anticipated. He sawed off the bone and discovered the infection was higher up in the leg, so he repeated the amputations several times. There was a lot of blood loss. When I finally had the chance to talk to my father, he was in a lot of pain but was very thankful for the hospital staff. My father told me he was awake during the surgery and could hear them sawing off his leg. He said he was in so much pain he couldn't move or speak, and had been really hoping to die during the procedure. I begged and offered to pay all expenses just so that the surgeon would keep him in the hospital until he was fully recovered. I was also buying time as it took me three weeks to find a good wheelchair for him in Cameroon.

By this time, everyone at my job could tell I was very distracted. I had been doing a lot of soul-searching. I had been procrastinating for several years about this big plan to return to my village and start a medical clinic. Now my father's ordeal instilled in me a renewed sense of urgency. I spent sleepless nights trying to figure out how I would accomplish my goal, and soon started calling all the influential Cameroonians I knew in the US. I wanted them to join me on this journey. The result wasn't very encouraging. Some promised to help but made no commitment, and a majority cautioned me that I was wasting my time and money. Some of them had tried projects in Cameroon and had failed, mostly because of the corruption and intimidation by government officials.

Initially I was discouraged as well, but not for long. If I put the people's interest first and God was my guide, no one would deter me. With all this newfound courage, I decided to tell my boss, Dr. George, my plan. My goal was to get more time off work to make annual mission trips to Cameroon. He told me he had just finished reading a book called *The Purpose-Driven Life* by Max Lucado. Dr. George wondered if he had missed the message from God due to his hectic neurosurgical practice. He said he knew he had saved many lives over his twenty years of practice, but if he hadn't been there, someone else would have done the job. He said if he lost his job or died, the hospital would easily hire another neurosurgeon. So what was his contribution to the world that only he truly could have done? I asked myself the same question. The next two months were a roller coaster of events that helped create what is now Purpose Medical Mission.

I received a call from my friend Mike Reddell who reminded me of his dream of one day taking his son to Africa. I had spent a year living with him, but he wanted to see where I was from. He knew I was passionate about my village. He wanted to be part of my first mission trip and eventually wanted to get his whole family involved. Another friend, Kathy Marcum, who was in the same PA class with us, was married to a pastor and through our days in PA school heard me talk about one day returning to Africa. She also wanted to join us. Then there was Dr. Sammy Deeb, a general surgeon who was one of my preceptors during my clinical rotations. He had also heard me talk about Cameroon several times. He was born in Syria and had lost his father at a very young age. He eventually moved to the US with his mother to pursue higher education. His uncle, a local cardiac surgeon, took care of them until he passed away when Sammy was in college. Sammy was now one of the most well-respected general surgeons in town and had always wanted to go back home to Syria to improve the health infrastructure, but as Christians growing up in Syria, they had always feared for their lives. When he heard about my plan, Dr. Deeb thought this may be his chance to fill the void that he didn't get to fill in Syria.

Also joining us was Dr. Shawn Conard, a graduate of the University of Kansas, whom I had met during my family medicine rotation in the rural town of Muleshoe, outside of Lubbock. He and his partners practiced true rural medicine: on any given day they faced a variety of problems, everything from common colds to farming accidents. They even performed simple to complex procedures, including surgeries such as C-sections and hemorrhoidectomies. Dr. Conard had been on several medical trips and encouraged me not to give up on my dream to return home to Cameroon. When his wife was pregnant with their second child, she had gone into premature labor and had been rushed to Lubbock. The baby stayed in the pediatric ICU for several weeks before discharge. I visited them several times and on one of those visits we talked about my plans. Despite his busy practice and two young babies at home, Dr. Conard told me he wanted to accompany me as well. Finally, my office nurse, Tonie Burkett, joined the mission as well. I had commitments from five American medical professionals. With their help and after several planning meetings, we decided our mission would involve erecting a building where we could see patients and perform minor procedures.

While building a team and a plan in the US, I was also in constant communication with the local leaders of my village and my father. Because Munyenge was without electricity or running water, they suggested that we put up the medical building in the town of Muyuka, the biggest town in the region where villagers routinely went for farming supplies and to sell products. My parents owned a two-acre piece of land at the edge of town, which they offered as the site of our first clinic in Cameroon.

So things were moving pretty fast, but I couldn't stop worrying about the possibility of something going wrong. Top among my concerns were corrupt government officials intimidating the farmers with requests for bribes. I was concerned that farmers might not know the right person to talk to about getting the necessary permits for this project. It was February 2008, and the trip was set for July. I contacted the mayor in Muyuka, the local priests, the commissioner of police, the divisional officer and many more local leaders to explain my plan. I could tell from my conversations with them that they had never been exposed to someone who was willing to help them without expecting some financial benefit. Many in the past who had made promises never fulfilled them and some had taken advantage of the farmers. Some had even extorted money from them without rendering services they had promised. The local leaders were very hopeful, but at the same time cautiously pessimistic. I felt it was imperative for me to make a quick trip to Cameroon to start putting things in place for our first mission campaign.

I bought a farm truck in Japan for my father, before his leg amputation.
He was never able to drive it.

My sisters inspected the piece of land in Muyuka that my parents
donated for the construction of the hospital.

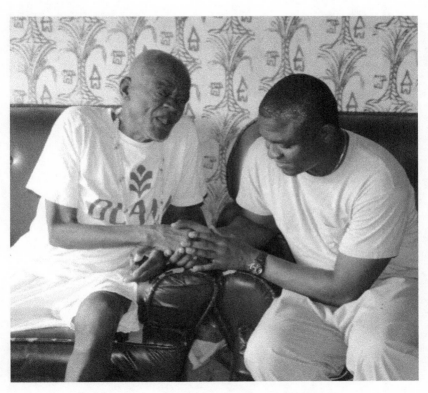

The talk. I asked for Dad's permission to marry Kyu Mee (1).

The talk. I asked for Dad's permission to marry Kyu Mee (2).

The talk. I asked for Dad's permission to marry Kyu Mee (3).

The talk. I asked for Dad's permission to marry Kyu Mee (4).

My Dad and me.

Kyu Mee and me in Maui, Hawaii, on our engagement day.

Our wedding day, in December 2008.

CHAPTER 10

JOURNEY TO PURPOSE

I DECIDED TO TRAVEL to Cameroon in March, four months ahead of the planned mission trip. With my friends and colleagues sacrificing their time, I had to do something to assure the success of our first mission trip. I also had enough money saved so the villagers could start building the first two-room clinic. While I was in Cameroon, I wanted to visit the Ministry of Public Health, as well as the government agencies involved in administering permits for such an undertaking. Again, I turned to several very successful US-Cameroonians to help me gain access to these agencies. I made several phone calls. Everyone seemed to want to know how he or she could become involved in the "business" and how they could profit from it.

Out of frustration, I made a plea to the American Embassy in Yaoundé, the capital city of Cameroon. Since I didn't know anyone with influence there, I decided to visit the website to find out who the ambassador was, plus the chief of missions and other embassy administrators. There were no email addresses for them, but I figured if I knew the first and last name, and they were employees of the US State Department, I probably could at least get an email through by using a hyperlink. It worked! The

day before I left Texas, I received an email from the secretary to
the US ambassador, letting me know that she received my email
and would love to help. She wanted to know my contact number
once I got to Cameroon. She advised that she was not sure if she
could help, but she was very excited that I was willing to do this.
I gave them my sister's cell phone number.

Once I arrived in Cameroon, my sister informed me that the
ambassador's office had called and given her an appointment date
for me to meet the Chief of Missions at the American embassy.
I spent my first night in Douala, and the next morning I took a
public bus for the five-hour ride to Yaoundé. The last time I was
at an American embassy had been in 1995 in Brazzaville, Congo,
to get my visa to study in the US. The experience this time was
a little different. I could only think of my rare opportunity for a
private visit with the American ambassador to discuss ways of
giving back to my people. The entire embassy staff seemed to
know that I was coming. I was treated like a celebrity, and I felt
very safe and secure. My visit with the ambassador was brief, but
I spent more time with the Chief of Missions (Chef de Mission),
who made one phone call that changed the entire trajectory of
the project. He called the Ministry of Public Health and was
immediately connected to the Minister's office, the same office I
had tried unsuccessfully for months to contact.

Within forty-five minutes, I was filling out the appropriate
forms and permits. Then a call was made on my behalf to the
Provincial Delegate of Health for the Southwest region, the
agency in charge of anything healthcare-related in my region
of the country. Finally, I was placed in touch with a man at the
Ministry of Health (MOH), Dr. Martin Monono, who told me he
would contact a friend who would definitely help. He got on the
phone and I heard him say, "Hello, John, I am sending you a
colleague from the US who needs some assistance helping our
people." When Dr. Monono got off the phone, I asked him who
"John" was and he said that Dr. John was one of his best students,
a good man who would be able to help me. It turned out that Dr.
John was the same physician who did my father's amputation.
He was very excited to find out I had come to help as promised.

That same night, I was invited to a dinner in my honor at the home of Justice Fobella. This high-ranking judge had invited several of his lofty government colleagues. During the meeting, the contingent apologized for the trouble I had encountered and thanked me for the undertaking. They offered to help if I ever needed any assistance. I knew exactly what this meant. In countries like Cameroon, it is very important to know people in high places if you plan to do almost any type of significant project. We exchanged phone numbers and promised to keep in touch. In all, I was in Yaounde for less than a day, and was eager to return to the Southwest Region to begin my work.

The next day I was in Buea and Muyuka where I was well received. The most important part of my message was that I wanted to help local officials build their own clinic, which they would manage. I could help them with maintenance and replenishment of supplies, and promised I would put in 100 percent, but they had to do the same, too. We wanted to help them take care of themselves to create a healthier and more hopeful society for their children. This became the heart of our organization's mission. But despite all the assurances, I knew executing the plan would be difficult.

If you have ever worked in a Third World country, you know nothing ever goes smoothly. And sure enough, there were many challenges, two that really tested my commitment for the project. As soon as I arrived in Buea, I was stonewalled by local delegates. I went to the hospital to meet Dr. John and told him of my frustration in trying to meet with the provincial delegate. He told me that the guy was a tyrant, an oppressor and a megalomaniac. I had heard this before, but now I was on the ground with just a few more days to go. After Dr. John's description, I really didn't want to meet the delegate, but I knew that he had the power to help or make life miserable for us, so I insisted on meeting him. Then, Dr. John found out that the governor of the province and the delegate of health would be attending the launch of a vaccination campaign in a nearby town. Our new plan would be to bypass the delegate and go straight to the governor at this event.

Dr. John canceled the rest of his day and we drove to the launch event in Muea. When we arrived, the place was crowded with locals in traditional attire with a lot of police security. Dr. John was well known by the villagers, so we managed to make our way all the way up to the podium where the officials were seated. We waited for our opportunity to meet the governor. It was a miserable forty-five minutes of unbearable heat, humidity and dust. I felt like everyone was staring at me because I was certainly out of place: I was dressed in jeans and a white T-shirt which at this time was more brown than white. After the occasion, there was a brief meet-and-greet. Dr. John held my hand like I was a baby and pulled me through the crowd. A police officer spotted me and put his hand on my chest to stop me from advancing. Dr. John told him that I was with him. So the officer smiled at Dr. John and opened the final path for us to meet the governor. Dr. John did a military salute without even making eye contact with the governor. The governor, in a broken English and a thick French accent, greeted Dr. John. The governor also welcomed me and, to my surprise, screamed loudly through the crowd to get the delegate's attention. The delegate walked over, and then stood at attention as if waiting for instructions. The governor introduced me and told the delegate to help me in any way he could. Then the governor walked away. I was now with the delegate and Dr. John.

As soon as the governor walked away, the scolding began. The delegate berated Dr. John for disrespecting him. Then he turned to me and said, "Who do you think you are to come to this country and bypass me?" He was visibly very upset. Then he said, "How would you like me coming to your country, America, and start doing things without getting permission from the people in charge?" I tried to explain that I had tried to reach him through emails, phone calls and personal contacts, all to no avail. He told me to "shut up" and said, "You will see," and then walked off. I looked at Dr. John in shock. All he could say to me was, "It's okay."

During our drive back to the hospital, Dr. John could tell that I was broken. He tried to convince me not to give up. He urged me to go to the village, and continue the plan of building the clinic, and putting things in order for the July mission trip. He would see what he could do. We decided that without the delegate's permission we could not open a clinic, but we could at least have annual short-term missions with the authority from the health minister's office. But I did not like this. My plan was to create something long term and sustainable. While I was running around the country trying to build a network of support, the villagers were actively building the structure for our first clinic. The Mayor of Muyuka and Nkem, my mother's brother, were in charge of the construction project.

Before I left for the airport to return to the US, I had a meeting with the local leaders who were very excited to hear about my trip and all the contacts I had made. During the meeting, a local chief announced that in my one week in Cameroon I had done what no one from our village had done in his lifetime. To them, the thought of ever meeting a minister or a governor was unimaginable. Now they felt empowered. One villager asked to shake my hand. He said he just wanted to shake the hand of someone who had shaken the hands of people who most likely to have shaken the hands of the president. They also encouraged me to keep pushing forward, despite my treatment by the delegate.

My second unfortunate event was more of a nightmare. Friday, March 21, was Good Friday. My flight out of Cameroon was scheduled for 11 PM. That day I spent the afternoon in Douala with my eldest sister and her family. I had been using her cell phone the entire time I was in Cameroon to make and receive calls. At around 7 p.m. we gathered the family in her living room to join me for my last meal before heading to the airport. I thanked everyone for their help and gave away all my personal belongings, including my clothes and shoes, to the neighborhood kids. My sister, her husband and I drove together to the airport. We said our goodbyes outside the airport and I handed back her phone and went through airport security. Once I was inside, there was no other way to contact them until I was back in the US.

The first police checkpoint was outside the airport. My luggage was searched and I stepped through a metal detector. The second checkpoint was inside the airport, and was designed to stop travelers from carrying any agricultural food products. I had none. This checkpoint was manned by plain-clothed city officials. If you have ever been to Cameroon, you are very familiar with this checkpoint. If you have food products, they charge you a fee to bring them—even though bringing food or plants without proper permits onto an international flight was illegal. Basically, it was a shakedown. I went through the third police checkpoint, the final stop before starting the airline check-in process. I stood in line with my luggage and waited my turn. As I approached the Air France passport control counter, the officer asked for my passport and told me to stand behind the line. He looked up at me and then called one of his colleagues. This was when I knew something wasn't right. The second officer asked me to step forward and away from the line. He ordered me to stay there until he returned. Then he walked away with my passport. No explanations were given to me.

The first officer took my bags and placed them behind the counter without looking at me or saying a word. I quietly stood while he processed other passengers. I waited for over twenty minutes before asking him what was going on. He looked at me briefly and said, "Your passport is invalid." I wasn't sure what that meant, so I asked. He angrily said I needed to wait for the second officer. For over forty-five minutes I stood there with my heart pounding and a million things going through my mind. Then the second officer returned, but this time he was accompanied by two police officers. One of the police officers had my passport in his hand. The security officer informed me that I would not be traveling and that I had an illegal passport. I was in such shock that I didn't know what to say. Everybody at the airport at this time was looking in my direction.

My passport had been issued ten years earlier in Cameroon. This is the passport I used to leave the country in 1995 and had used on several international travels without any problems. In fact, I used the passport through all security checkpoints for the trip home. The police officers told me to grab my bags and follow them. We went through the crowded area towards the back of the airport into a dark hallway to an isolated room at the very back of the airport. During our walk, I tried to talk to the officers, but they said to hold the explanation for their boss. They opened the door to a room, and both of them did their routine military salute to a morbidly obese man sitting behind a very large desk. He was in full police uniform with four gold stars on his uniform above each shoulder. I knew that he was the commissioner of the police force or in the French Le Commissaire de Police. His back was toward us as he talked on the phone and worked on a laptop on another smaller desk behind his chair. As he turned to face us, one of the police officers handed him my passport and, in French, explained that Air France security had "spotted" me with a passport that was invalid because page twenty-eight was missing. The commissioner then turned toward me and asked if I had any explanation for carrying a "fake" passport. He told me that a page had been torn out of the passport, which usually meant someone was trying to hide something or the passport was illegally made. I spent another thirty minutes with them screaming at me to tell them where I got the passport and threatening me with jail.

At one point, one of the officers took me outside the room and asked me if I had any money to offer the commissioner to let me go. I reached in my pocket and showed him that all I had was 20,000 francs CFA, the equivalent of $40. I had given away all the money I had except 10,000 francs to pay the mandatory airport fee, and another 10,000 francs to keep "just in case." He told me that I was headed to jail unless I could come up with at least 50,000 francs.

In my desperate attempt to explain to them why I was in Cameroon, I mentioned that I had visited the US embassy and several government officials. I pulled out the names and phone numbers of the people I had met. Immediately, the mood in the room changed. I said if they could get me a phone, I could call one of these officials to back my story. He wouldn't let me use a phone, but instead handed me my passport and asked if I had a family member who could come pick me up. He instructed me that if I promised never to talk about what had just happened in his office, he would give me his phone to call my sister. I agreed. The other two officers abruptly left the room as if they didn't want me to know their names. The commissioner handed me his phone. Before dialing the numbers, I looked at the time on his phone and realized that my flight had already left.

As soon as my sister heard my voice she knew something had gone wrong. I just told her that I was okay and asked how I could get back home. She told me to take a taxi and tell the taxi driver to take me to a gas station close to their house where they would be waiting for me. It was almost 1 AM, and it would take another two hours to get a taxi at this time of the night. I spent that time going through the pages of my passport to see what exactly they were talking about. Indeed, page twenty-eight was torn out.

A few minutes after my phone call, a different police officer came to the commissioner's office to take me outside where I sat, waiting. This time, the police officer was English-speaking and from my part of the country. He listened to my ordeal and at least acted empathetic. He told me that one of two things must have happened. First, he believed that this being Good Friday, a lot of wealthy Cameroonians and Air France employees like to travel to France for Easter holidays. Also, the President of the country had declared the Monday after Easter to be a holiday, which gave everyone in the country an extended Easter break. They would typically pay the security officers to find reasons to detain passengers, which would then open seats for these "standby" travelers. He believed that the security guard tore my passport. The second, less likely, possibility was that a jealous family member or friend had done this to me. But it didn't matter at this point. All I could think of was what to do now that my passport was invalid. There were no taxis available. As I was waiting I saw a private vehicle drive up to drop someone at the airport. I approached the driver and asked if he would take me to the gas station, which was on the other side of the city. I offered him all the 20,000 francs I had, and he agreed.

When I finally reunited with my sister in the middle of the night, I could tell she had been crying. She, too, thought my passport must have been torn by someone at the airport. I stayed up all night waiting for sunrise to start calling all my newly forged contacts to see who could help me get a new passport. They all told me that the process normally takes up to three months. With high ranking connections, it could take a week or two. I must have called more than a hundred leads, all to no avail. Some people asked for money and others just gave me another number to call. I was willing to pay whatever it took just to get out of the country. I had never wanted to leave a place this badly before. Finally, I received a call from Dr. Ekokobe

Martin. I had met him during my dinner in Yaounde and knew that he worked for the police department at the capital city. He told me to come see him in Yaounde on Monday and he would see what he could do on Tuesday. Since Monday was a holiday, no government offices were opened.

I spent the weekend notifying people in the US that I would not be coming as expected. Everyone was very concerned. Of course, Kyu Mee was beside herself. I tried to sugarcoat the problem when I spoke to her, and promised to call her on Tuesday. I told God that He would have to show me more than a miracle if this project was what He wanted of me. If so, why was this so difficult?

On Easter Sunday, I reluctantly went to church with my sister's family. She had talked to her pastor about my ordeal. I believe the sermon that day was urgently changed to address my situation. It seemed that God was speaking directly to me through Pastor Sam. There was laying of hands on me by the entire congregation, and washing me with the blood of Jesus. There couldn't have been a better day for the message. The pastor came to me after church and asked me to think of Jesus's suffering and His death for my sake. Then he reminded me that today we are celebrating His resurrection. I reminded myself that nothing worth fighting for has ever come easy for me, and that God will never give me more than I can handle. So with every setback, I grew more resilient.

Monday couldn't come fast enough. I traveled via public bus and spent the night at Dr. Ekokobe's house. He left for the office very early the next morning. He took my invalid passport with him and asked his wife to bring me to his office at 9 a.m. This is when the miracle began. His wife led me up to his office. When I got there, there was a police officer waiting for me. Dr. Ekokobe gave him money and instructed him to take me to a nearby photo shop to get a passport photo. He also handed me a copy of a passport application form to fill out. We went downstairs to the lobby of the National Central Police Department. I spent the next two hours listening to him apologize to me for what had happened. It was then that I found out that he was a physician and one of the highest ranking officers in the police force. In fact, he was the personal physician to many military leaders including the Minister of Defense. He was doing all this for me, free of charge. He was pessimistic about the healthcare situation in Cameroon, especially in the southwest region where he, too, was from. His hope was that he could also open a clinic in this region after his retirement.

While we were talking, the police officer arrived with a brown manila envelope, and handed it to him. Dr. Ekokobe opened the envelope and handed me a dark green passport. I saw my new picture engraved in the leaflet unlike the old passport where the picture was glued to the page. I was in tears. I asked him how much I owed him, but he told me to hold the thought, because the day wasn't over yet. He asked me if I was interested in traveling on the same day. I didn't think that was even possible. He reached for his phone and dialed a number. He explained my situation to the person on the line. He hung up the phone, again reached in his briefcase and this time handed a handful of money to the officer and told him to use his car and drive to the Air France travel agency. There, I received an itinerary to travel that same night from Yaounde through Douala, then Paris, Houston and finally Lubbock. He promised me that my stop in Douala was just to get more passengers. I arrived in Lubbock on Wednesday, March 26.

Once back in Lubbock, after recovering from the trauma of my trip, I was able to regain strength and resolve by communicating with my new friends in Cameroon, and my friends in Lubbock who, even after hearing my story, still insisted on going with me. Then, a month after I left Cameroon, my eldest sister called me one night to inform me that her husband, whom I stayed with in Douala, had suffered a stroke and was taken to the hospital. He died while waiting in line for a CT scan of his brain. While in Cameroon the previous month, I had diagnosed him with hypertension and told him that he needed to visit his doctor. I had promised to bring him antihypertensive medications on our July trip. This was a devastating and senseless loss to our family, especially my sister and my niece, their only child. During the mourning process, Kyu Mee and I decided we would go ahead with our plan of opening the clinic in Muyuka. We were not going to let anyone or anything stop us.

At the Vaccination Campaign in Muea, we waited to meet the Governor.

At the Vaccination Campaign. Dancing for the Governor.

My brother-in-law, Christopher, helping with the construction of the
Healing Touch Hospital in Muyuka.

Vaccination Campaign.

Visiting the US Embassy in Yaounde.

CHAPTER 11

THE HEALING TOUCH

OUR FIRST TRIP WAS filled with emotion. It had been thirteen years since I left Cameroon. My father had a dream: he had planted in my head that he would like to see a medical facility in our area before he died. After years of watching his children, friends and family suffer from illnesses, he believed it was necessary. He just didn't realize it would take him losing his leg for this to finally happen. In any case, the dream was becoming reality, and he was alive to see it even if from a wheelchair.

I left Lubbock with six friends: Rick, the neurosurgeon; Sammy, the general surgeon; Mike, the emergency room physician assistant; Shawn, the general practitioner; Kathy, the internal medicine physician assistant; and Tonie, the nurse. None of them had ever been to Africa, and some had never been outside the US. I spent plenty of time talking to them about expectations, the culture, the people, the food, the village, and my family. I must admit that even I didn't know what to expect. Nothing I said would have prepared them for what they were about to see.

I had hired a driver and a Toyota passenger van to pick us up at the airport and take us to and from the clinic. We traveled up to Buea overnight. I did this because the temperature in Buea is more moderate than that of Muyuka. The next morning we got up very early to unpack our supplies and started making our way down the mountain to the clinic in Muyuka. My sister, who accompanied the bus driver, warned us that everyone in the surrounding community was very excited about our arrival and there were some surprises for us. It was the talk of the town and surrounding villages.

We arrived at the clinic to see many people, including patients, construction workers and curious villagers, lined up. Our first surprise was that the two-room model building we had paid for had already expanded to a seven-room facility. The facility was made up of three buildings housing a triage area, examination rooms, a laboratory, and three patient wards—one for children, one for men and one for women. There was a room for the doctor's office, and a minor procedure room. We still did not have a doctor for the clinic, but our plans involved working with several doctors to see who would be best suited to take over and help run the clinic.

The local leaders named the clinic, appropriately, Healing Touch Medical Center. Kyu Mee and I paid for most of the building construction. With the help of my colleagues in Texas, we organized a fundraising event in our office parking lot to raise additional money for the building. We raised $900 from friends lining up to participate in a pie-throwing contest. Friends and co-workers would pay a donation to line up and throw a pie at either me or Dr. George's face. The event was sponsored by Peoples Bank, a local bank in Texas managed by another friend. My father and the mayor of my village had also made separate donations once they realized that the original place was not going to be big enough. Some of the work was still ongoing, but we had the room to carry out our campaign. The second surprise was that the chiefs and leaders of all the villages had planned a welcome ceremony for us with food, drinks, speeches and traditional dancers.

Hundreds of patients showed up each day of our visit. We treated illnesses ranging from minor farming accidents, arthritis and hypertension, to typhoid, malaria and diabetes. With our handheld diagnostic tools, we were able to diagnose many patients with severe undiagnosed hypertension and diabetes. Patients came from distant villages to see us. Most of them had never seen a doctor. They were very thankful and some even brought us food and gifts. For the patients who needed surgery, we transported them to the provincial hospital in Buea where my father had his leg amputated. We performed several procedures with Dr. John, who was very excited to share his operating room with the "American doctors." We worked side by side with the local doctors and nurses who came out to volunteer with us.

My family was and still is very involved in the mission. My father came down from the village (Munyenge) and stayed in a rented house across from the clinic. He would visit and pray with us every morning before work began. During the day he would ask to be brought to the clinic. He would sit in his wheelchair at the front entrance and greet patients as they walked in or out of the clinic. My mother stayed in the same rental house with him. Daily, she would prepare our lunch and would make sure we take a lunch break to eat. She also would make water rounds, as she was worried we would get dehydrated, and that my white friends would die from the 100-plus Fahrenheit temperatures. We had no air conditioning or fans. Indeed, two of my colleagues felt sick, one from the heat and the other from a gastrointestinal ailment.

My sisters and the volunteer nurses all helped with triage. Some of the patients arrived at the hospital as early as 3 a.m. to make sure they or their children were seen. Some patients were brought in on makeshift wooden stretchers and some wrapped in clothes for transportation. We saw things that even I had never seen before, injuries that had been abandoned for lack of care. We saw a farmer who had a fractured *humerus* (arm bone) that had occurred fourteen years earlier. He came in for knee pain, but we couldn't help but notice that his arm was dangling beside his body. The fracture had never healed and so the bone was completely separated. He was in no pain and didn't want us to do anything about it. We saw people who had lost their eyesight and limbs from accidents. We saw people with gastrointestinal worms and patients seizing right in front of us. At times, it seemed like we were in a war zone. For the local people, it was just everyday life.

One that hit me personally was a kid I knew. He grew up in my neighborhood. His mother brought him in to see if we could help. He had fallen off a coconut tree and was rendered completely paralyzed. He could move his head from his neck, but nothing else. His family carried him all the way to us. I recognized him while his mother was telling me his story. As a neurosurgery physician assistant, I knew his fate. He wasn't going to make it. He was already covered in pressure sores and wounds after only two months out from his injury. We told the family that there was nothing we could do. They asked us to pray with them and thanked us for taking the time to look at him. His mother went on to tell me how much they appreciated me for coming back. She said now they can have a healthier life. I couldn't get over the fact that her only son was dying and the mother still expressed appreciation.

Three months prior to the mission, we sent a shipping container from the US that held supplies for the new medical clinic. While working at the hospital, we had a team of local leaders led by a military captain who were in Douala trying to get out our twenty-foot shipping container that was still at the port. On day two in Cameroon, we had to take a break to travel to Douala after news reached us that the container had cleared customs and that we needed to come pay the final fees to release and transport it to the village. After the release, the container was safely transported to Muyuka. We were able to help set up the rooms and train the staff on the use of all the supplies we had brought, most of which were foreign to them.

By the end of the mission, everyone was physically and emotionally exhausted. We were without a doubt overwhelmed by the need. There were many patients who we could only pray with, as we knew we couldn't help and most likely they would not be alive by the next year's mission trip—if we ever came back.

Our last stop of our mission was Saint Joseph College, Sasse, the secondary school I had attended. Even though my experience there was horrendous, I wanted to make sure I helped in any way possible to ensure that their students were receiving better care than I had. I had been in communication with the principal who welcomed us to the campus. When we visited, I found that the sick bay was just like I had left it. The principal told me that they didn't have funding for the medical supplies. We toured the sick bay, which this time was a different building. There were no mattresses on the beds or basic first aid supplies. With the help

of my team, I was able to take the school a truckload of much-
needed supplies, including mattresses, wound care supplies and
basic medical equipment.

The two-week trip was so draining I was convinced that my
friends would never be returning. I thought they had seen too
much suffering. But after a very emotional last-day meeting
during which no one could keep their emotions in check, they
were more committed than ever to not only return, but to help
create a sustainable long-lasting model for the community. Before
we left, I took the team to visit my family and my home village
of Munyenge. We also got to meet a group of handicapped men,
women and children who all came to meet us. My father had
founded and sponsored an organization in the village to support
the handicapped. He told me that he believed God took his leg
so that he could see what the disabled people went through and
better understand how he could help.

Sammy, Mike and I traveled to the capital city of Yaounde
after seeing the other members of the team off at the airport in
Douala. We wanted to give a personal report to the government
officials who had worked relentlessly against all odds to make our
first mission possible. That night we were hosted to dinner with
all the officials who were eager to hear our story. We spent most
of the evening discussing our findings, the diseases we treated and
how much help we needed from them to make our mission truly
sustainable. Most of them admitted that, despite their assistance,
they were still skeptical of our motives. No one does anything
without seeking some kind of financial reward, they said. I again
reiterated that our mission was unlike many others. We were just
representing a group of West Texans who had heard my story and
wanted to help. We wanted nothing in return but a better life for
the people.

I told them of my unsuccessful attempt to get the regional
delegate on our side. One of the representatives from the Minister's
office promised to follow up on that issue. We would find out later
that the regional delegate lost his job about a month after our
visit. Dr. John, my father's physician, would be appointed the
regional delegate of health for that region. This could just have
been coincidental, but the news was well received.

Donating supplies for the sick bay at Sasse College.

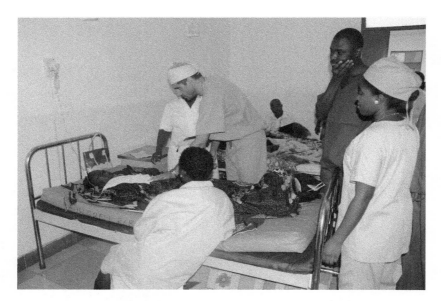

Dr. Deeb with medical students in Cameroon doing morning
rounds on post-surgical patients.

Family members bringing my father to Healing Touch Hospital, Muyuka.

First fundraising event. Dr. Rick George covered with pie.

First trip in 2008 with Military Captain Fortaboh,
who was instrumental in the success of the trip.

Healing Touch Hospital dedication with village leaders.

My father, with the administration of the Disabled People Association of Munyenge
which he founded after his leg amputation.

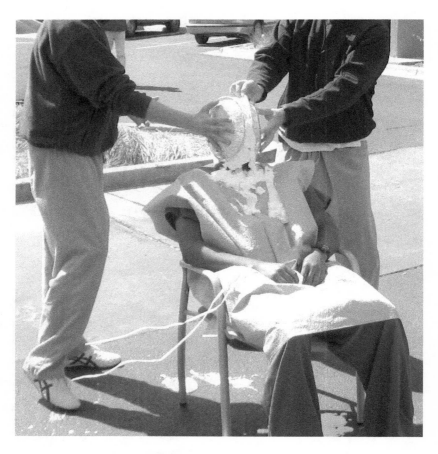

Pie-throwing fundraising event. That's me under all the pie.

Planting dedication trees at Healing Touch Hospital, at the end of our first mission trip.

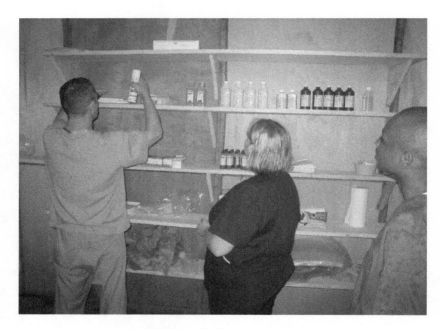

Setting up the clinic before our departure.

The chief of Muyuka cut the ribbon to officially open
Healing Touch Hospital in Muyuka, Cameroon.

I visited Sasse College in 2008 to donate supplies for the sick bay.

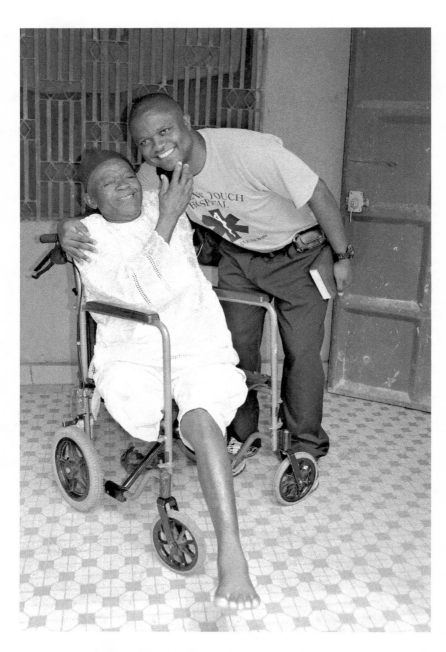

With my father during our first mission trip in 2008.

CHAPTER 12

PURPOSE MEDICAL MISSION

WITHIN WEEKS OF OUR return, the news of our mission spread in Lubbock, as the team of volunteers shared their stories. I started getting calls from people all over West Texas who wanted to contribute to the mission or were interested in going on a mission trip. Since I hadn't planned on getting the public involved, I had no way of accepting donations. Dr. Sammy Deeb also informed me he was getting donation offers as well. We decided to form a nonprofit organization to broaden our reach and enable us to accept contributions. In the meantime, another nonprofit organization founded by a local physician, Dr. Kyle Sheets, would accept donations that were intended for our mission work in Cameroon.

Creating a 501c organization initially sounded very simple until I started reading about the rules, the need for a board, a mission statement and strict accountability standards. I also looked at how much it would cost to get a lawyer involved. It wasn't cheap. I reached out to a Cameroonian-born American attorney. Also I met with the colleagues who visited Cameroon on our previous mission trip for recommendations. We had our first meeting in October, 2008 to come up with a mission and vision statement, and also decide what type of organization we wanted to create.

Dr. James Burke, an orthopedic surgeon originally from England, had joined the core group. His wife was from East Africa. He had heard about the need for orthopedic services in Cameroon, and was already committed to going with us the following year. It was a very productive meeting as we all were familiar with the people and the goals of the organization. We agreed that there had to be very strict accountability. Dr. Richard George was elected chairman of the board, Mike Reddell as vice chairman, Dr. Sammy Deeb as the medical director, Kathy Marcum as treasurer, Dr. Burke as the advisor, and Julius Lyonga, a colleague from Cameroon, as the Cameroon liaison. All board members were volunteers with no financial compensation or incentives. Every volunteer would pay his or her own way, unless sponsored by another individual or organization. We wanted to ensure from the outset that all donations were used directly for medical projects. There would be no paid staff members. We decided the organization had to be different from other missions in that anywhere we decided to work, the goal would be to create a sustainable model enabling locals to utilize the healthcare facilities we would build or supply. That meant focusing on educating the local people and then expanding or improving whatever medical infrastructure was already in place. Our job would be to empower people to take control of their destiny. It is commonly said that if you teach someone how to fish and give them the tools, they will never go hungry. If you feed them without showing them how to get their food, they will go hungry waiting for you to bring them food. Teaching the local community how to sustain their healthcare was our number one priority.

Once our mission and mode of operating were agreed upon, it was time to get it back to the lawyer. I anxiously awaited his email response. Finally, I received a postal mail from him. In it, he sent a personal letter listing some demands in return for his services. I read it in utter disappointment: he had agreed to file the documents for us but asked that I write a letter acknowledging that he was part of the mission, and was providing his services free of charge. That was fine, except he wanted me to circulate the letter to village leaders to make sure he received credit for his contribution. I wasn't sure exactly why he needed this, but I knew that it went against everything I believed in. I always wanted the villagers to take ownership of the project—not me or the board. Our mission was always about them, not us.

At first, I didn't want to share the letter with our new board for fear of discouraging them. But then I thought they needed to know all the challenges we were about to face if we were going to embark on this journey together. When I shared this with our newly elected board, they were disappointed but determined to move on. Dr. Sammy Deeb called a local Lubbock lawyer on the spot and wrote her a check for $1,500 for filing services. We were now a legal entity.

Purpose Medical Mission was formed to be a bridge of medical assistance to severely medically underserved communities around the world. We picked the name "Purpose" because we all believed that this was a call from God to be an extension of His healing touch. At the very core of our new organization's mission was a belief in partnering with the people we serve to make sustainable positive impacts in their lives. We would work alongside them and help create a community that believes in serving one another in the name of Christ. We are united in His body and serve Him by serving each other. Our goal was to develop a bridge of assistance from West Texas and the US, and extend God's love to the far corners of the globe.

After the creation of the organization, we started planning for the second mission trip to Cameroon, to be in 2009. We had promised the people that we would return. The clinic there continued to grow during this time. They had hired a local Cameroon physician who moved to Muyuka and worked full time at the clinic. They had hired four nurses, several nurse's aides and a custodian. The goal of our 2009 trip would be to equip the hospital with medical and surgical supplies, build an operating theatre that could be used for more complicated surgeries by us and the local physician, to equip the hospital with an ambulance that could transport patients to larger hospitals for cases they couldn't handle, and also to have a transportation van that we would use while on the annual trips. Clinically, we focused on preventive medicine and prenatal care.

All the local hospitals in Lubbock got involved. First, Covenant Health System's CEO signed a waiver that gave us full access to their storage facility. University Medical Center would also help with donation of surgical supplies. The Heart Hospital would donate boxes of medical and wound care supplies, and enough scrubs to last a lifetime. Grace Clinic would donate an anesthesia machine and anesthesia medications for surgeries we planned to perform. Then, I received a call from the widow of a doctor who had passed away several years ago. Mrs. Bayouth had a warehouse full of physical examination tables and all supplies needed to open a new clinic. She and her sons, David and Charlie, would spend an entire day going through the supplies and help me load them into the storage facility in preparation for shipment to Cameroon. Dr. George would buy an ambulance on eBay for $5,000 from a guy in Connecticut and have it transported to Texas. It seemed the entire city of Lubbock was involved in the mission. My phone was ringing nonstop.

The next big idea involved non-medical-oriented business. Engineers would get involved, as well as plumbers, welders and construction businesses. The local news networks, such as Fox and ABC, would also help with outreach and fundraising. At the same time, I was communicating with the construction crew and hospital administration in Cameroon to make sure everything was going as planned. I also arranged to purchase a 40-foot container for loading and shipment. With the help of many local volunteers, we were able to successfully load and ship our second container to Cameroon.

In July of 2009, I travelled with eleven volunteers to Cameroon. As expected, the people came out in droves. We had a clinical and education team in Muyuka and a surgical team in Buea. We immediately found that the small operating room was too primitive for complex operations. The construction crew in Muyuka had built a small ten-by-eleven-foot room with no water or reliable electricity. So, all the surgical patients were asked to go to Buea, but most of the patients couldn't afford public transportation to make the thirty-mile trip to the city. We had to fix that situation.

Our container was still at the port in Douala awaiting clearance. After each day, we would get news that, for one reason or another, we needed to pay more money to get the container cleared. We were getting very frustrated because our van, ambulance and most of the supplies sat at the port in the container. Still, for the first two days we kept working. On the third day, before beginning work, we were invited to the governor's office for a meet-and-greet. After visiting with the governor, we met with the governor's assistant, who was on our surgery schedule from the previous day, but had to be postponed due to our lack of supplies. We informed him about the container. He told us that the only thing the customs officers were interested in was obtaining bribes, or hoping we left the country without clearing the container. They were stalling so they could confiscate the van, ambulance and other supplies, and then auction them off. I informed him that I had arranged the entire process of shipping the container legally and by the book, so I shouldn't have to pay bribes. He laughed and addressed me as "brother." Then he said if I didn't pay the bribe, the container would never leave the port. Hearing this, on our way back to the hospital, we decided to cancel all surgical procedures and send a team to Douala to demand the release of our container. As soon as we made the announcement to the crowd, there was an outcry from all who had travelled from faraway places to see us. Then the patients started voicing their support for us. They were all willing to do whatever it took to show their support for us, and their disappointment in the government who, they believed, should have done everything in their power to assist us.

We soon were visited by several local radio stations, newspaper and TV stations in the region. Then my phone started ringing. I got calls from the chief of customs and other government officials who advised me to travel to Douala and collect our container. Three of my team members accompanied me to Douala, where we spent two days going from one office to another getting documents signed, and eventually got the release of our supplies and cargo without us paying a dime of bribes. Throughout this process, we would network with more officials who would prove very instrumental in the success of this mission for years to come.

We eventually got the supplies to Muyuka and set up the hospital before departing. We were also able to perform all the planned procedures. I was able to be part of an answered prayer and help fulfill a promise I made to my friend Mike Reddell. His wife, Donna, the wound care nurse, and his only son, West, accompanied us and were instrumental in the success of the 2009 trip. Donna was able to work with the local nurses to set up the only wound care center in the region.

We had been using a generator for electricity, and water was carried from the nearby stream. With the help of the local officials in 2010, we got electricity expanded into the clinic. They also extended water lines to the area and into our hospital, which became a fully functional medical facility in the region, serving a population of over 16,000 people and treating about 5,000 patients a year. Since most of the patients still couldn't afford to go to the provincial hospital for more serious illnesses, we decided to expand and upgrade the facility with patient wards, a diagnostic department, and labor and delivery room. Upgrading the operating room would prove to be a challenge.

The initial overwhelming consensus was that we in the US would design and finance construction of the operating room, for the locals in Cameroon to build. The idea was that the operating room would have its own independent, uninterrupted electricity and water supply. We feared that electricity would go off in the middle of a procedure, which was very common with the local energy grid. We involved several local electricians and engineers in the planning. They couldn't agree on how we could convert their electricity grid to power our equipment without destroying our instruments. Like in the US operating rooms, we needed a backup generator in case we lost power.

During our many planning meetings, Dr. Burke asked the engineers about the feasibility of building the operating room in the US and shipping it to Cameroon. This way, we could guarantee the sterility, water line, air conditioning, and electricity supply. *How in the world do you ship an operating room?* Then he mentioned that the US Army at one time had built mobile clinics made out of shipping containers. We could get two shipping containers and place them side by side, then cut out doors, electrical outlets, plumbing and air-conditioning to the outside. We would then construct a model operating room. After construction, we could load the containers with medical supplies for shipment. The local construction team in Cameroon would build the foundation for the containers. Once the containers arrived in Cameroon, a team of engineers from Lubbock would travel to the site to put the two containers together and then connect all the lines to the generator and water service. This was a novel idea, but we had to make sure it could be done.

We discovered that Lubbock Christian University was doing similar projects and building dormitories out of shipping containers. We contacted their project manager who not only was willing to offer his services, but also was very excited to be part of the project. He asked for a tour of a typical operating room (OR) in the hospital. One night after work, a group of us suited him up and gave him a tour of the OR. Within weeks he was given permission by the school administrator to utilize their resources and manpower for the project. Most of his construction guys also volunteered their time towards the project. We started by purchasing two forty-foot containers and placed them side-by-side on the Lubbock Christian University parking lot. With the help of several construction teams, the project was completed in three months. Then in May 2010, a team of seven volunteer contractors travelled with me to Cameroon to put the operating room together. These were not medical practitioners—they were plumbers, welders, joiners and electricians—from all over West Texas, paying their own way and offering their services free of charge to help people on the other side of the world. The entire assembly took four days. Once the technical part was done, local carpenters built a complete building around the operating room to protect and secure it.

In July of 2010, a team of twenty medical providers and evangelists travelled to Cameroon. We performed thirty-two surgeries and consulted on over a thousand patients. We also performed the first total hip replacement surgery in Buea, and the first spinal surgery that had ever been performed in this part of the country. This was done in the operating room we built out of shipping containers. The education team focused on health awareness, especially HIV prevention. The evangelistic team visited and preached at several local churches while distributing Bibles and praying with patients at the hospitals.

Over the next three years we would help expand the hospital to include a second Operating room (OR), an X-ray department, and pediatric and adult wards. In 2013, we successfully installed a water filtration system in the hospital in Muyuka to provide clean drinking water to the patients and people in the community. In 2016, a second clinic was built in Cameroon.

Despite the hospital in Muyuka, most people in my village and other places outside Muyuka still couldn't afford to travel to Muyuka for medical treatment. After a thorough feasibility study, the decision was made to build a satellite clinic in my home village of Munyenge. After three years of raising funds and working with the villagers, the facility was officially opened in 2016. The facility was built on the same two acres my father donated for a clinic before my initial trip to the US. It was his dream to see a medical clinic in our village to treat the locals. Unfortunately, he wasn't there to see its opening. The ribbon-cutting ceremony was performed by the chief of Munyenge. It was the first fully functional medical clinic ever built in my village.

This dream was made possible by the hard work and dedication of many individuals in Cameroon and in the United States, especially Crissy Haralson and Nicole Hines. These two ladies in Lubbock approached us in 2009 and asked to help with our fundraising efforts. They both have planned our annual fundraising events which have allowed us to make even bigger contributions not only in Cameroon, but in other communities around the world. Their commitment to our organization has been unparalleled as we seek to bring healthcare and better quality of life to very impoverished parts of Africa and Central America.

Adult health education class at the clinic in Munyenge.

Ambulance being removed from the shipping container.

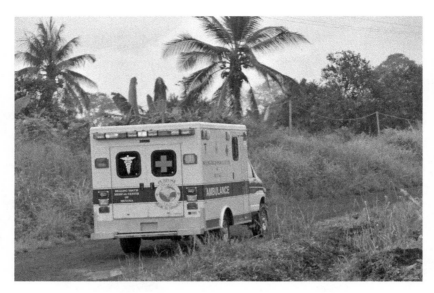

Ambulance we purchased on ebay and shipped to Cameroon,
on its first patient transport trip from Muyuka.

Container operating
room completed, with air
conditioning unit attached.

Container operating
room is loaded with
medical supplies after
construction.

Current board of directors of Purpose Medical Mission.

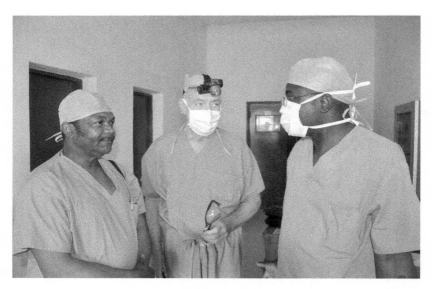

Dr. Burke consulting with two other othopaedic surgeons,
Dr. Mbako (England) and Dr. Fokam (Cameroon).

At their lodging, Dr. Fokam, Dr. George, Dr. Burke and PA Mike
review cases the night before surgery.

First hip replacement surgery.

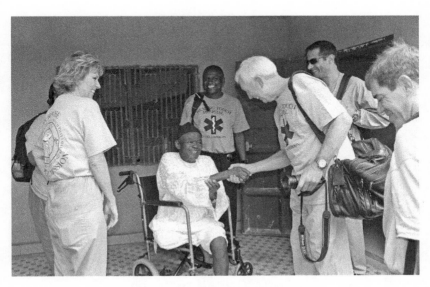

Introducing the team of volunteers to my father.

Mike, Donna and West Reddell at the Muyuka hospital in 2009.

Opening day of the Munyenge clinic.

Operating room containers are assembled in Muyuka.

Operating room shipping containers arrive Muyuka.

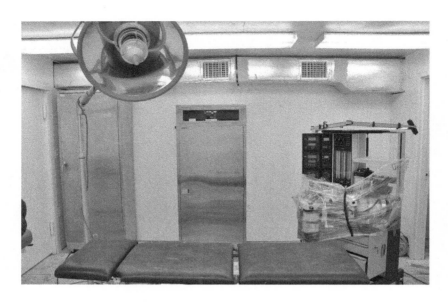

Operating room containers are assembled in Muyuka.

Operating room project in Lubbock.

Operating room project. Shipping containers ready for shipment.

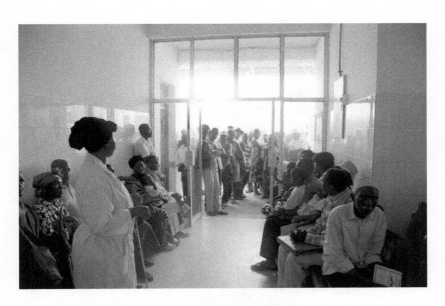

In the halls at the Provincial Hospital in Buea, patients line up for consultation.

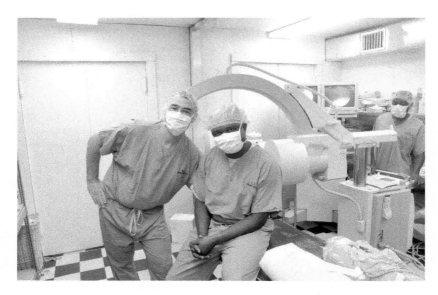

Preparing for first spinal surgery at Healing Touch Hospital in Muyuka.

Students in Lubbock volunteer to load supplies for shipment to Cameroon.

Taking a break from surgeries to inspect the hospital expansion at
Healing Touch Hospital in Muyuka.

The chiefs of Munyenge and Lilale (neighboring village) cut the ribbon
to officially open the clinic in my village.

The new patient postoperative ward at Healing Touch Hospital in Muyuka.

The operating room arriving in Muyuka, Cameroon.

With my father on our second mission trip to Cameroon.

With village leaders at the opening of the clinic in Munyenge.

Collecting supplies from several hospitals in West Texas.

CHAPTER 13

PURPOSEFUL
MEDICINE

WITH THE SUCCESS OF the Cameroon project, we started receiving requests from individuals who wanted to join Purpose Medical Mission. At the same time, we were approached by several local and international organizations wishing to assist. As a board, we decided that for every invitation received, we would first send an exploratory team to evaluate the need and possibility of developing reliable relationships with the community and its leaders. The first of these missions was to the Central American country of Guatemala.

Martin Nowlin, an associate at a local investment firm in Lubbock, introduced us to Guatemala. Martin found out about us through a discussion with one of our board members, David Bayouth. David informed Martin that we had several people who wanted to volunteer with Purpose Medical Mission, but who could not afford travel to Cameroon, so if there was a place closer by, or an established organization that we felt had similar goals and mission with us, we could tap those willing volunteers.

Martin was a childhood friend of Mark Lanier, a Houston-based attorney. Mark was born and raised in the Lubbock area and attended the Texas Tech law school. Mark was widely recognized as one of the top and most influential legal minds in the US. His law practice focused on cases of injustice against individuals and corporations. He was also an avid theologian and teacher of the biblical literacy. I was privileged to meet Mark in 2010 at a fundraising event. Prior to the event, I attended Mark's Bible study class at his local church in Houston. I must admit that, prior to meeting him, my perception of lawyers was not very good. My first encounter with a lawyer had been in 1998 when I was involved in a car accident in the Dallas area. I was not injured, but a lawyer tried to persuade me to lie about my injuries for the purpose of getting more money out of an insurance company. My second encounter had been with a lawyer who promised to help with the formation of our organization but who wanted to take all the credit for the work.

I was impressed with how Mark applied biblical teachings to today's world. He successfully explained to us that being a Christian should be a way of life, not something we do once in a while. At the end of the class, he asked everyone to commit to doing a random act of kindness and declining credit or thanks. He said, "Just do it and walk away." What impressed me the most was that in my short time with him, I was convinced that not only did he believe it, he practiced unrequited kindness with his family and strangers. At Mark's fundraising event, we met Rose who had heard about us and was very eager to introduce us to her organization, Guatemala Sana. She was eager to see how we could work together.

Guatemala Sana is an organization founded by Dr. Rafael Espada, a Guatemala-born Houston-based cardiothoracic surgeon. After many years of a very successful practice at Baylor in Houston, Dr. Espada decided he wanted to use his skills and blessings to improve the quality of life of his people in Guatemala. He founded Guatemala Sana, whose mission was to provide high-quality healthcare programs to rural Guatemala. After retirement, he moved back to his home country and was elected the country's vice president.

Rose, who worked for Dr. Espada in Houston, became passionate about Guatemala. She quit her job of more than twenty years to help manage his organization. After we met her in Houston and learned of her story, the Purpose Medical Mission board agreed to send an exploratory team to Guatemala. I travelled with David Bayouth, a close friend and local business owner, Dr. Sammy Deeb, and Dr. Richard George, both board members. Once in Guatemala, we met with Dr. Espada and Rose who showed us the facilities they had built to administer care to the patients. We also met with the mayor and town leaders of Santa Maria de Jesus, where the Guatemala Clinic was located. After four days in Guatemala, we were moved by the impact the organization had had in the rural communities they served.

What was most touching to me were the sacrifices Rose made daily and the challenges she faced. Here was a lady who was born and raised in the US, had a successful job, and sacrificed it all to move and live amongst the people she was trying to help. I was reminded of the same sacrifice that Foculare Movement volunteers made to help educate me and bring healthcare to my ancestral village in Cameroon. And just like the Focolare Movement in Fontem, the clinic in Guatemala would expand to include an elementary school.

With the help of Rose, our first two mission trips to Guatemala were resounding successes. We spent a long time selecting volunteers who shared our goal of treating common illnesses, but most importantly educating the locals on basic preventive care. We spent our time at the Guatemala Sana clinic mobilizing surrounding villagers who hand-picked local leaders to join us to be trained on basic first aid, safe delivery practices, water treatments and basic hygiene. Board member Nicole Hines worked tirelessly to create and organize the education materials in Spanish that we handed out to the local leaders. These leaders would then return to their villages with supplies, and with the knowledge they needed to care for their populations. They would then be supported by the clinic in Santa Maria. These missions were so successful in the villages that Guatemala Sana asked us to send a second team yearly, to focus on prevention and medical education. This, of course, is a success story and you can see how the goals of this organization fall directly in line with ours.

Not all our exploratory missions have produced favorable findings as they did in Cameroon and Guatemala. In 2012, after an invitation, we sent a team to explore the feasibility of expanding our mission to Mexico. The organization there was having difficulties attracting patients to their free clinic. Unfortunately, after studying the work on the ground by the organization that invited us, we felt it did not match our mission. The US-based organization had built a beautiful facility in a rural village, much bigger and better equipped than the Healing Touch hospital in Muyuka and the Guatemala Sana Clinic in Santa Maria de Jesus. But the problem was that the Mexican facility relied too heavily on visiting volunteers from the US to keep it running, so the locals were not invested in the growth or future of the facility. They viewed it as an American hospital with American doctors coming to provide free healthcare when they could. The people did not trust the intentions of the organization, which emphasized converting the Christian locals to their particular Protestant denomination.

A few years later, we became involved with a mission in the Democratic Republic of Congo, which had been founded in 1951 as a seminary by missionaries from the United Methodist Church. The missionaries had been on the ground ever since the founding. Some of their children were born in the town of Mulungwishi, about 100 miles northwest of Lubumbashi, the second largest city in the country. There was a small clinic that needed our assistance to expand, and it was the only medical care in the region. We were especially impressed at how the missionaries had become part of the community. They sponsored a local student to go to medical school, to then return to their community to become their doctor. Over three years, we have sent doctors, engineers and construction workers to Mulungwishi to expand and train the clinic staff. They not only had a better and bigger clinic as a result, but a functioning operating room as well.

One of our most recent projects was in Los Altos, Nicaragua. We were introduced to the people of Los Altos by Jose Paniagua. This is a community of indigenous Nicaraguans who were displaced by the 1972 earthquake that destroyed the capital city of Managua. Jose was born and grew up in Nicaragua. He migrated to the US as a young boy after the Nicaraguan revolutionary war. He had done many short-term mission trips to Nicaragua, but wanted something more sustainable. He reached out to us, and again we sent out an exploratory team. During our first year, we carried out a medical campaign to identify the main medical ailments plaguing the population. We also visited with the villagers to hear about their needs. It was very similar to Cameroon. What they needed the most was a facility for the treatment of chronic illnesses such as hypertension and diabetes. Education was also going to be one of our biggest priorities.

In September 2017, after four years of planning and developing a relationship between us, the villagers and the government officials, we were able to successfully establish a fully functional clinic in Los Altos, Masaya, Nicaragua. It took many mission trips to understand the medical needs of the community, and they now have a clinic with two locally trained physicians.

We are always open to opportunities to help anywhere around the world, even in the US. We were heartbroken by the suffering of our fellow Texans in the aftermath of Hurricane Harvey in 2017. In the early days of the disaster, we reached out to several organizations that were already on the ground in the Houston area. Initially, we prayerfully made a financial donation to assist one of the local churches that was being used as a shelter. Then we received a call from the American Red Cross with an urgent need for durable medical equipment for the functionally disabled population displaced by the hurricane. We immediateley emptied our warehouse and delivered the supplies to Houston. Shortly thereafter, we were contacted for similar items at the Dallas Convention Center. This time we decided to reach out to the Lubbock community through social media and word of mouth. The response was immediate. Within two days, we were able collect over thirty wheelchairs, hundreds of walking canes, sixty-five commodes, and several boxes of general hygeine products. We transported and delivered the supplies to the American Red Cross at the Kay Bailey Hutchinson Convention Center. We could appreciate how much these items were needed, as they were put to use straight out of our trailer.

Construction of the Los Altos, Nicaragua clinic.

First Medical Mission trip to Nicaragua.

Hurricane Harvey relief.

Working with the team at the government-owned clinic in Osteonal, Nicaragua.

CHAPTER 14

PURPOSEFUL CHARITY

I AM BY NO means criticizing the godly works of other organizations. Any act that is intended to help another person is always good. Because I am someone who has been on the receiving end of charity, and now find myself on the giving end, consider this my attempt to influence how collectively we can use charity to foster human dignity. Ask yourself how the person you are helping feels about asking for your help. Then ask yourself how you can help get them out of that situation. What if you took a moment to ask yourself what got the other person in that position in the first place? I have been at that lowest place where I am at the mercy of the person I am requesting help from. Many people came into my life and were curious enough to ask me how I got here and where I was headed. They gave me that extra push I needed to get to my destination. They didn't say to me, don't worry about your sufferings, I got it from here.

So, what is charity? Many people will tell you that charity is voluntarily helping someone with nothing in return. I beg to differ. Let's be honest; we get something in return. Sometimes we get more than we give. When you offer to help someone, the fulfillment you get from doing the act can't be measured. There is no value to it. And the more you give of yourself, the more fulfilled you are. No one knows how long that fulfillment lasts. But what if you were to give something that truly keeps on giving? What if you gave something that gets the other person what they need in the short term, and continues to give long after you are gone, something that doesn't stop in your absence and doesn't wait for your next visit? This is what I call purposeful charity. It's giving with purpose to help you and others get to a destination. To help you find your own way of giving.

I found my way of giving through the people and organization that helped me along the way. This is what Purpose Medical Mission is all about. When we travel to some of the most remote places on earth, I am reminded of what that means to us and the people we are trying to help. We are perfect strangers driven by faith to perfect the body of Christ by helping one another. The people we are helping, in their own eyes, have done nothing to deserve our help. Most of them we will never see again. They have no way of ever repaying us. However, when we sit with them, pray with them, eat with them, laugh with them, the message they take back to their villages is of perfect strangers who loved them so much that they would leave their families, risking their lives to care for them.

When we work alongside them to build their own clinics and teach them how to care for each other, we are telling them that we expect them to care for themselves. The message I always leave behind is that if the volunteers I bring with me can care for them without knowing them, then God is asking them to care for each other. Show love for each other. Help each other get to their destinations, to fulfill their God-given purpose. This form of charity is most beneficial when dealing with the health or education of a group or community, the two aspects of life that I personally feel that every living person on earth deserves to have access to.

I am often asked how I managed to control my emotions on these missions when I am surrounded by so much suffering. I have had people tell me that they couldn't go to Africa because they are afraid it would be too depressing. The answer is simple: don't see the people as victims, see them as partners. We need them as much as they need us. This partnership begins from day one when we ask them how we can help. We need them to give us directions on how they want us to get involved. It is always very important for me to know what and with whom I am dealing. It's the most important predictor of the survival and sustainability of the project. What are their expectations of us? And what are our expectations of them? This must be very clear from the outset. It's more than just knowing that there is a need. There are needs everywhere in the world, but where can I have the most long-term impact in a community? We must make sure we are treating the right problem. If it doesn't work, we have to be willing to change the plan.

Don't just assume that you know the real problem of the community. If you are going to commit resources, make sure it solves the problem. Sometimes the solution to the problem may be as easy as you saying no, like we did in Mexico. Ideally, you are able to tell them why you can't help. If your relationship with the people you are trying to help is based on mutual respect and understanding, you will find out that your work will impact more than just their health. By working with them, you can help restore and protect what is important to them. If not, you potentially make the situation worse by imposing what you think is important to them.

In Cameroon, for instance, I quickly realized that not much had changed in all my years of being away, except that the people had given up waiting for their government to fix their problems. In my opinion, the government placed no value on the life of its citizens, unless the citizen was a government official. The people had no access to the government. One of the first things I had to do was forge a relationship with government officials for the purpose of getting some basic resources to the people I intended to help. It paid dividends. First, with the help of the government we were able to get permits for them to have a clinic and also find a doctor for the clinic. Prior to our coming, this was close to impossible to do. We were also able to develop an effective line of communication between us, the government officials and the locals. When you have a trilateral line of communication, especially in Third World countries, it's easy to detect a fallout or disconnect in projects.

None of our missions have been without obstacles. In Nicaragua for example, the trip to open the clinic in 2017 was challenging but a blessing in disguise. A local news organization from Lubbock was sending their news anchor with our team to cover the story. We had arranged for two travel teams to go to Nicaragua. I was part of the first team. We left three days prior to the grand opening date, to help set up the clinic and meet with our partners in Nicaragua who would be running the clinic after our departure. The second team was made up of the news anchor, Bryan Mudd, and Dr. Burke, the orthopedic surgeon and a board member. Bryan had never been outside the US, but Dr. Burke was well traveled and had been to Cameroon on five separate mission trips.

Upon their arrival, Bryan's television equipment was confiscated at the airport and held with demands for payment for some "special permit" to film. After several negotiations the news crew was asked to come back to the airport the following day—the day of the grand opening. Dr. Burke and Bryan traveled overnight from Managua, the capital city, to Masaya where we anxiously waited for them. When they arrived, I could tell that something was wrong. Bryan was visibly angry and disappointed. After hearing their story, Dr. Burke and I calmed him down by making him a drink. We tried to amuse him by telling stories of worse encounters in Cameroon when Dr. Burke and I had spent several days in the port city of Douala with no change of clothes, trying to get our shipping container out of the port. While we did this, Jose, our Nicaraguan liaison, was on the phone calling all our high-ranking contacts in Masaya and Managua to work on getting the camera and TV equipment released. It was diplomacy at its best.

Just like in Cameroon, we engaged the village leaders to put pressure on the government officials as well. The following day, we had the opening ceremony with some of the most colorful performances by the villagers, but without Bryan's high-definition equipment to record the event. However, at the end of the day, we received a message from a high-ranking military official to send a team to Managua to collect the equipment. We didn't pay a dime. The rest of the trip went perfectly, just as planned. We were able to set up a governing board for the clinic made up of two local physicians, the village leader, the head of the construction crew, and a retired military colonel.

On the final day, while reflecting on the trip, I told the team that the trip couldn't have gone any better. We had a news organization that came to cover the grand opening of our newest clinic, but instead they got the entire Purpose Medical Mission story, including our incredible day-to-day challenges.

Health education of children is key.

Meeting with the village leaders of Los Altos, Nicaragua on our second trip.

Our second team to Guatemala is pictured here with
Vice President Rafael Espada at the Santa Maria de Jesus clinic.

Partnering with the people we serve.

Patients show their appreciation after consultation.

These traditional garments were handmade by villagers in appreciation for the volunteers.

The Fon (King) of my ancestral village presents a gift of appreciation
to Chiara Lubich and the Focolare movement in Fontem.

The grand opening of the Los Altos, Nicaragua clinic in 2017.

The US-and-Cameroon combined construction crew,
praying after the completion of the container operating room project.

The village of Osteonal, Nicaragua during our first feasibility study trip.

Vice President Espada introducing our team to the people of Guatemala.

Village leaders from the Santa Maria de Jesus area are given certificates after completing the health education program prepared by Nicole Hines and Elena Caudle.

Visiting with government officials in Nicaragua.

Visiting with villagers in Los Altos, Nicaragua.

Volunteer electricians working with the locals in
Mulungwishi, Democratic Republic of Congo.

Working with local medical providers in Democratic Republic of Congo.

CHAPTER 15

HOPE VERSUS DESPAIR

WHAT IS HOPE? IF you perform an internet or a dictionary search, you will find hundreds of different definitions. What I am referring to is "an optimistic state of mind that is based on an expectation of positive outcomes with respect to events and circumstances in one's life or the world at large."

As a Christian, I believe that if we trust in God, He will answer our prayers. Only He can make those dreams come true. Both the Old and the New Testaments contain many verses and stories about the importance of hope. We are taught that if we want something, we must be willing to endure trials and tribulations, and if we obey His commands He will see us through. Yes, we have to work for it. The most inspirational of these stories to me is The Exodus, the story of Moses and the Israelites. It's the story of how the Jewish people were delivered from years of slavery to the land that God had promised them.

Moses was entrusted with the responsibility of leading the people through the wilderness to Mount Sinai, where God would reveal Himself to them and then give them His commandments, the laws by which they should live their lives. If they would follow these laws, then He would take them to their promised land. They doubted Him many times through the journey and disobeyed Him. Several times during the journey they would turn away from God and His commandments. In the end, it would take forty years, a second generation and a different leader before the Israelites finally made it to Canaan. I think about this quite frequently.

My father always talked to us about hope in terms of its Biblical meanings, how God took the Israelites from slavery and provided them hope. My father reiterated to me that it took a lot of sacrifice for them to see their dream land. He also spent a lot of time talking about what happens to a society when there is no hope, such as the despair and hopelessness over the political situation in Cameroon. These conversations were usually with Dad's fellow farmers while they were working, or in the evenings after a long day when his friends would stop by to visit. It was the driving force behind his decision to sacrifice his life and belongings to give me and my siblings a decent education. Hope is what has sustained me since the day I arrived in the US without anything but my name.

Once I arrived, I started to notice why the United States is so successful. It's because of hope. Almost everything about the society is designed with the future in mind. Higher education, research and entrepreneurship are all highly encouraged and supported. The Constitution of the country is open for everyone to see and is regarded as sacred. People freely talk about their goals and hopes for a better future. This is especially evident during elections, when people can espouse their views without fear of persecution. This is not the case in most developing countries.

In the US, if you need something such as a driver's license, there are clear requirements and fees—not bribes. If you meet those requirements and pay the fee, no one can stop you from obtaining a license. And if they do, there are laws in place to protect your rights. In most developing countries, this is not always the case. Just knowing how to get information is a daunting task. And once you get the information and meet the requirements, it is still not guaranteed you will get what you seek. At the risk of going on a tangent, I will take a moment to describe my experiences and concerns about Third World countries, especially my beloved Cameroon.

The most dreadful thing that one human being can to do to another is to take away their hope, or intentionally prevent them from attaining their full potential. This happens every day around the world, especially in Africa, where the only way to maintain power and control of the people or the country's resources is to deprive the people of their God-given rights to control their own destiny. These governments and leaders pretend to care for the citizens and then control every aspect of their lives.

I have had the privilege of visiting Cameroon at least once a year for the past ten years. What I have observed is quite honestly a complete disappointment. Year after year I see the physical and moral infrastructure of the country collapsing. In fact, it appears to be moving backwards. There is widespread corruption that has metastasized into every aspect of the people's lives. It stems from the highest levels of government where corrupt officials use public funds to enrich themselves and their friends at the expense of the civilians. It's a place where retired workers give up hope after bribing at different levels to collect their hard-earned pensions; a place where senior government officials fly to foreign countries to seek medical care while most of the population doesn't even have care for their most basic health needs. Some civilians feel that they have to bribe healthcare professionals just to see a medical provider. There is complete lack of respect for free speech or human rights.

Every year as I travel around Cameroon, I meet citizens and government officials who lament on the state of their government but are terrified of expressing this in public. Currently, the young, vibrant population is migrating out of the country at an alarming rate. In fact, on my last count, more than half of my high school graduating class have already emigrated. The youth are dying to cross oceans and deserts to reach Europe, Asia, the Middle East. Even the people who limit themselves to their villages for fear of governmental control cannot avoid the reach of government corruption.

My parents and most farmers work from dawn to dusk to produce cash crops to provide for their families. Each year, after months of hard work, they are faced with price-fixing by the agents of government officials who work as middlemen and keep all the profits. The farmers have no control or access to the free market. They are left with no option but to take whatever price is offered them, which is typically a fraction of the actual value of the crops. They are not even allowed to make inquiries about the market value, and what little money they get is often taken from them by corrupt officials.

I vividly remember when I was twelve years old my parents were encouraged during a government campaign to use a newly opened bank called Cameroon Bank for their savings. The government was teaching the citizens how to save money for their children's future. The farmers were asked to entrust the nationally owned bank with their savings. Most of the farmers had been keeping their money at home. Many took all their savings and deposited it in this bank. One morning, news went across the village that the bank had closed, and all the bank managers had left. No explanations were given. The farmers waited for months, but to this date we still have no idea what happened, and they never got their monies back.

The young adults whose parents, like mine, sacrificed everything, are still graduating from Cameroon universities without jobs. Those willing to try and find a job have to go through reams of bureaucratic red tape, and many ultimately give up. People bribe just to get jobs. And if you get a job, sometimes you have to pay a bribe just to collect a salary. The people are intimidated at every stage of the process, an ordeal so exhausting that most people just give up trying. Today, I see a desperate society where people have been broken by their own system. The situation is made worse by a government that takes advantage of the people's desperation and fear to tighten its control.

I have to say that my biggest challenge in Cameroon over the last ten years has been trying to bring positive change in an environment that is incredibly corrupt. Obviously, not every official is on the take. But corruption is pervasive.

The day we went to open the first clinic in Cameroon, I was summoned to the office of the Special Branch Police Station. It was in the middle of the day, at our busiest time caring for patients. I had never heard of a police unit called Special Branch. I initially hesitated, but I was advised to go. It was explained to me that they were an elite police unit that reported directly to the president of the country. When I got there, the director of the office spent over thirty minutes, when I could have been treating patients, to tell me how important he was and how he could help me get all the documents needed for the clinic. Then he told me that his job was to guarantee my safety. I asked him what I could do for him. He told me that typically people give him 10,000 Francs per person visiting, but because I was doing God's work, my fee was 5,000 Francs per volunteer. I didn't want to argue with him and indeed needed to get back to the clinic, so I handed him 50,000 Francs, the equivalent of $100. He took the money and then started talking to me about his wife who was a "highly" trained midwife. He wanted me to hire her. This was presented more as a threat. I told him that I didn't control who was hired at the clinic but that I would let the hospital administration know. In fact, not only did we not hire the wife (whom I later found out had no formal training), I informed the hospital administrators that if they hired her it would be a big mistake. These people hounded the hospital administration for years until they finally gave up.

Once, we had to temporarily shut down the hospital because government officials would randomly show up with demands for money, such as the taxation office and social security (CNPS) who would threaten to close the hospital unless they were paid. They threatened and badgered hospital administrators until they were paid extortion bribes. These same types of things happened to my father when he opened a small shop in the village, when I was just a boy. I remember many times when the government officials would show up asking for money, and he would hand them all his profits just to keep the shop opened. All his businesses failed for that reason. Father was always outraged by this, but felt that because of his lack of education, he was handicapped from imposing any change or defending himself. He encouraged us to never to be afraid to impact positive change in any community, because at the end of the day good and evil will always clash and good would prevail. Unfortunately, he never saw this change happen in his lifetime, and I may not in mine either, but I will keep talking about it for anyone willing to listen.

I fully understand how grim my assessment of Cameroon sounds. However, I say this because of my unbreakable love for this country and its people. They are all victims of a corrupt system. Why else would I leave the comfort of my home in the United States, sacrifice my financial resources, jeopardize my job or be gone for an extended period of time from my wife and my children? Because of my love for the people and my hope for a better future. I just chose to use medicine to change my community because that is my calling.

I never lose sight of what my work means to the people I interact with on my mission trips, especially in my hometown. I see hope in the people's eyes when I visit Cameroon. Every year, I am surrounded by family members, friends who I grew up with, young children, and parents of these children. I have had countless conversations with them. I have come to realize that they see in me more than a medical provider. I hear the parents telling the kids that I was one of them, and if they study hard they, too, can be like me. The kids love to just come and hang out around the clinic while we work. In me they see hope that is reachable, not something farfetched, hope that is not just a story of a distant individual. I am one of them.

Every year, when we visit Cameroon for a medical mission, it has become a tradition and my way of showing my appreciation, to spend the last full day seeing the countryside. My colleagues are always amazed by the beauty of the country. You can travel from the desert through a temperate climate to the rainforest, all in a day. In less than an hour, you can travel from the highest mountain in West Africa, with an active volcano, to swimming in the Atlantic Ocean. I typically get comments like, "This place looks just like the scenes from the *Jurassic Park* movie." During a drive, there is a request about every five minutes to stop for pictures. Then there are the security officers stopping us to tell us that we are not allowed to take pictures, especially around the properties owned by the government, such as the country's oil refinery, which is located in an area surrounded by several very poor villages near the town of Limbe, in the South West region of the country. The land is extremely fertile and the views are spectacular, a tourist heaven. I see unending potential in the country.

With all the above-mentioned challenges, our mission has managed to survive and will continue to thrive because of some incredibly honest and God-fearing government officials who have taken the time to listen and get to understand what we are all about. From different sectors, we have received assistance which has allowed us to continue to bring hope and healing to the people most in need.

Through our work we have experienced confessions and changes of heart as well. I will share with you a very personal experience from one of my trips to Cameroon. While driving from one town to another, I was stopped by a police officer who said he just wanted to inform me that my very close family member was in jail. He explained to me that the family member had been in jail for three days without any visitors. He was arrested for apparently wrecking another person's car and had no money to pay for damages. He would only be released if he paid the sum of two million Francs (approximately $4,000). Against the advice of several family members who were convinced that this was a scam, I visited the family member in prison to see for myself. It was indeed true that he had been arrested. I was told by the police officer on duty that I had to visit with the police commissioner to make arrangements for his release. His wife did not have the money to pay, and I certainly didn't either. However, when I visited with the commissioner he suggested that I take a loan or use collateral, and if I didn't pay, the collateral would become the property of the government. I informed him that I had no property in Cameroon and hence had no collateral.

During this conversation in the commissioner's office, I realized from his line of questioning that he had no idea who I was. I then interrupted him just to introduce myself and explain why I was in the country. He remembered that my team had taken care of his very sick daughter on a previous trip. He gave me a stern look, then walked over to close the door to his office so no one outside could hear the rest of our conversation. He then confessed that my family member had come to him with a business proposal. Upon finding out that I would be in Cameroon, they had planned for the family member to be arrested and tortured to extort money from me. They would then split the money amongst all the players.

After the confession, the commissioner sent one of his officers to bring the family member into his office, with me still present. Not knowing that the commissioner had revealed their scheme, the family member begged me to help get him released. He showed me all his bruises from being beaten in jail. The commissioner then slapped him across the face and asked him why he hadn't told him who I was. He started screaming profanities at my family member, telling him that he was "a bad person" for getting him involved in this plan. Then he walked towards me and asked me to forgive him. I was speechless and walked out of the office, never looking back.

I have been held by security officers several times for the most insane reasons, such as taking pictures of beautiful scenery just because it was near the oil refinery. Once, I was held and asked to pay a fine to the police officer because we took a picture of young men diving from their boats into the River Mongo to collect sand. The divers would go underwater for over a minute, then come back up with a large bucket of sand. I was detained because the bridge was a sensitive security location connecting two parts of the country. In this case, I had to call a higher ranking police officer to be released. These are officers I knew, and some we had treated as patients. The sad truth is that the government is so paranoid about the possibility of an uprising that they resort to terrorizing their own citizens. They do not even trust each other. Some of the few good leaders have been corrupted or forced to comply with the status quo. Again, we were blessed to have a few important government allies, otherwise our mission in Cameroon would not have lasted a year.

I am still hopeful that there will be a change of hearts on a larger scale, and that our children can one day visit and maybe live in a free and fair Cameroon where hard work and honesty will be respected, and people will have a government that truly cares for the well-being of its citizens. There is evil everywhere we go, especially when the devil promises us material possessions and worldly riches, but we are called to always speak the truth and help transform evil into goodness. We are asked to take a stand against the evil of corruption, embezzlement and lies. In a place where paranoia by the government and distrust by the people clash on a daily basis, there is a risk that people's rights will be violated. The popular saying in Cameroon is that you can always bribe yourself out of any situation. In my attempt to be part of the solution, I adopted a "no-bribing" policy about nine years ago after our first mission trip when we were constantly approached with requests for bribes. For me, that has proven successful. For everything I do, I work with the appropriate officials to get the right permits or documents. This process itself is daunting as you always discover a new policy every day. Regardless, I notice that you are typically left alone once the authorities realize that you are familiar with this system. Unfortunately, when I advise other Cameroonians to adopt a similar policy, I always get the comical response that it wouldn't matter. Documents or no documents, you are still expected to "feed" the officials to get anything done. There is some truth to this as even when I do my very best to abide by the laws, I frequently still have to contact higher-ranking officials to get things done. I still think that if everyone would just stop condoning these habits, there is a chance we might turn the tide. It would depend greatly on the government taking the first step to end corruption and then pay the salaries of those officials, so they are not forced to intimidate their citizens for bribes. I pray that the government can find a way of creating a society where the truth is allowed to be heard.

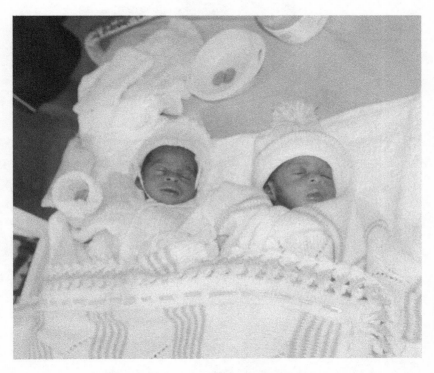

A hopeful future. Twins delivered at Healing Touch Hospital by the local doctors.

A typical car wash in my region of Cameroon.

After days of relentless work, our shipping container
was released by the Cameroon customs.

Beautiful Cameroon coastline.

Beautiful Cameroon.

Children playing in front of the hospital while we work.

Children returning home carrying produce from the farm.

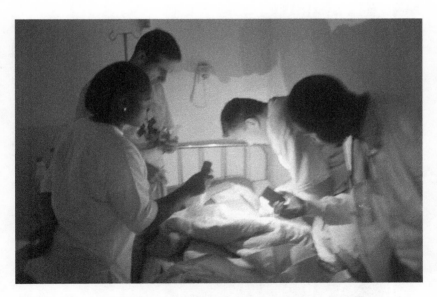

Dr. Deeb and anesthesiologist Dr. Rob Minielly check on a postoperative patient at the Provincial Hospital in Buea. We used our cell phones for light after the electricity went out.

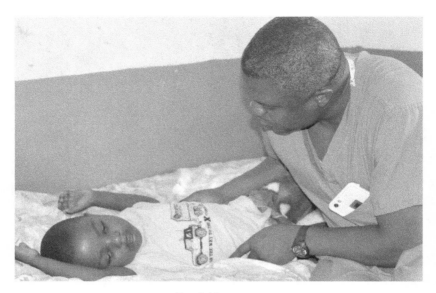

Hopeful Cameroon.

Kids playing in front of the hospital.

Many government officials who have helped to make our mission successful.

Meeting with Cameroon government officials in Yaounde, after our first mission trip.

Mount Cameroon is the tallest mountain in West Africa.

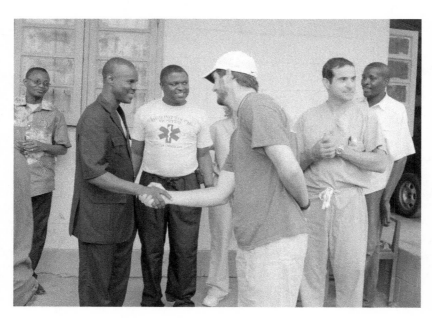

The Divisional Officer of Muyuka Sub-division who
helped during the initial phase of our project.

The road to Munyenge today is worse than it was 24 years ago.

CHAPTER 16

THE AMERICAN "DREAM"

"AMERICA, THE LAND OF milk and honey, the place where money falls off trees for anyone to grab. All you have to do is make it to America, and you will become rich." These are the things we heard about the United States from scores of Third World people longing for a better life. It should be no surprise to us then that people are dying to cross deserts and oceans to come to this great nation.

In my opinion, there is no other country on this earth better than the United States. It allows everyone, regardless of class or financial status, the opportunity to achieve their fullest potential. We all have our opinions about America's politics, race relations, or religious tolerance. However, if one is willing and able to invest the time and energy, he or she will succeed in the US. Obviously, there are circumstances that can prevent individuals from attaining success, but in relative terms, and from my personal experience, most immigrants in today's America can be successful. However, they must put in the work it takes to achieve success.

America is not a country for the weak or lazy. If you are the get-rich-fast type, the system will chew you up and spit you right back out. It is not a perfect country, but it's the one country that encourages its citizens to keep striving for greatness. So, yes, there is plenty of money and material possessions for everyone, but an understanding of how the system works is key to achieving a true American Dream.

When I ask people what the American Dream means, most immigrants typically talk about owning a big house and driving that "dream" car. And if material possessions are a scorecard, then almost every immigrant I know has achieved some degree of success.

I understand that the whole idea of the American Dream means something different to different people, usually based on their upbringing and exposure to hardship or a life of luxury. Since arriving in the US more than two decades ago, I have had several family members follow under my sponsorship. Two of them have lived with me and my family while pursuing their education. My wife and I took care of their basic needs and tuition. We helped with that first car, taught them how to drive and even helped them get that first job. They never had to worry about where their meals would come from. They never had to stand out in the scorching heat of the summers or blinding cold weather of the winter season for hours to hitch a ride from a stranger after work or from school. They never had to be gone from the apartment for days so that they could pick up extra shifts at different job sites. And if they needed anything, they had a cell phone to dial our numbers.

I am happy to have helped family members. And, as a result, their idea of the American Dream most likely will be different from mine. I am now raising two boys who will never go through my life experiences. My point is that what most people consider the American Dream is influenced by our past experiences, and can also be influenced by material possessions.

We get excited about that big house or that fancy car that we feel we deserve after many years of education or our personal hardships. In fact, in my experience people live and die in debt. When I talk to friends and colleagues about debt, the typical response is that no one in America will ever be debt-free. One friend actually told me that it is patriotic to be in debt as the American financial system would collapse if everyone in America were debt-free. Hence, we get very cozy with credit card debt, thirty-year home mortgages loans and never-ending car loans.

In Cameroon, especially in my village, it is not uncommon to see multiple unfinished houses with people living in them. A family would gather their money from their farm harvest and buy their lot. Then they work on the building plans while saving for the next step. Once they have enough money, they could start building the house. The family builds in a manner that allows them to move in while the house is under construction. This could take several years, depending on the finances. There were no banks to borrow money from, not in the villages. You could participate in what we called "njangi," where a group of people came together and contributed a certain amount of money into a "pot" to be picked by each member once a month. That is, if there are twelve members and everyone contributes one hundred dollars a month, then each month a different member goes home with $1,200 until everyone has benefited. If you don't pay you can be certain that everyone in town will find out, and good luck ever trying to borrow from anyone or be part of a njangi group again.

Despite my experiences during my first few years in America, I was also influenced by how easy getting credit and accumulating wealth seemed to come in the US. I was exposed to the fancy cars by wealthier friends, and soon started thinking of the American Dream in terms of what I had and what people saw. A fancy car is a status symbol. Expensive clothing and shoes make you appear rich. Boy, was I wrong. Thankfully, my first major mistake happened early on in my American experience and would help define my idea of the American Dream.

Soon after arriving, I quickly found out that owning a car in the US was a necessity, not only for the rich as was the case in Cameroon. In fact, everyone in college is expected to own a car. I did not know of a single university student in Cameroon who owned a motorcycle, let alone a car. My first year I lived on campus, so there was not a need for a car. Almost all my classmates had cars. They would frequently invite me to take rides to Walmart on the weekends to get school supplies. They would also invite me to their houses for holidays where I would see that everyone in a household owned a car. My second year, when I now could work and start saving money to buy my own car, I either walked to school or begged for rides daily. I also paid for people to take me to my job. At the end of my second year, I bought my first car with cash through an auction. This car did not last long. In my third year, when I was shuffling multiple jobs and school, I needed a more reliable car.

My big mistake came after I lost my first car. One of my uncle's friends who worked for a dealership in Dallas told me that I didn't need money to get a car. He said I could simply walked into his dealership, sign a few papers and drive off with any car I wanted. I trusted him. So one day he picked me up at my apartment and drove me to the dealership. He spoke to the manager on my behalf to get me the "family deal," supposedly reserved only for families of employees. I must say, it was the best customer service I had ever had. The sales manager met me at the door and took me straight to see the perfect car he had picked out just for me. It was a nine-year-old beautiful blue Mitsubishi Eclipse, the model where the headlights popped out of the car when you needed lights. I tried to ask the price of the car, but I was told they would do whatever it took to make the price right for me.

Finally, after hours of my friend begging the manager to make me a deal, I was told that the car was only going to cost me a $380 monthly payment. I didn't know anything about principal, interest, or the terms of monthly payment. They already knew how much I made each month, and told me that I certainly could afford that on my nurse's aide/teaching assistant/grocery store cashier salary. We drove the car on Highway 75 in Dallas. It was a beauty. I went into the office and signed the paperwork and they handed the keys to me. Oh wait, I needed full coverage insurance from another friend of the manager whose office was just across the street. With the keys in my hands, signing up for insurance was a no-brainer. Long story short, when I started paying for the car loan, my payment including insurance was over $600 a month.

After nine months of driving this car I could hardly afford to pay for my rent or my college tuition. I found myself picking up shifts at the nursing homes every weekend just to keep up with my bills. My grades were slipping. My priorities had shifted to keeping up with my car payments. I called the dealership and credit union where the car was financed to ask them to help me figure what options I had, but no one was willing to help me. They said if I didn't make the payments, the car would be repossessed and that would affect my credit for the rest of my life. I had no way out. I researched repossession and decided that I would rather go back to a life without a car than sink deeper into this dark hole with no hope of ever getting out.

Per my research, it would affect my credit but at least I could get a clean slate after seven years. I stopped making payments, hoping they would come get their car. Every day after work or school, I would clean out the car, knowing they would show up in the middle of the night to get it. I would wake up every day, disappointed that the car was still there. This went on for over three months. Then one afternoon, after working the night shift and going to school that morning, I came home to take a quick nap. After getting ready to go to my other job in a neighboring town, I noticed the car was gone. I stood outside my apartment for a few minutes to process what had just happened, then went back in and called my job to tell them I wouldn't be making it. I then took another refreshing nap and turned the page on to a new chapter. It felt as if a very heavy weight had been lifted off my shoulders. I had learned a lot through this process. I told myself that this would never happen to me again.

My next car was a thirteen-year-old Mazda 626. I was at a dealership in Arlington, Texas with a friend who was looking into buying a car. I can't remember why I went to the back of the dealership where they had several junk cars that were not for sale. I went in and asked the salesperson that my friend was working with if the car was for sale. He told me that the car was involved in an accident and had been totaled by the insurance company. They were waiting to take it to an auction to sell it for parts. I asked if we could see if it's running. He spoke to the manager and got the keys. The manager said he would sell it to me for $750 cash, but I had to sign a few waivers saying that I knew the car was junk and that they would not be liable for anything whatsoever. I bought the car with cash and took it to my apartment complex. I knew a Vietnamese family in Grand Prairie that owned an auto body shop. I gave them my last $300 to get the car ready for inspection. I owned this car from 1999 to around 2010, and took it to the mechanic just for oil changes and basic repairs. Though some of the parts of the car were held together with coat hangers, I never had any mechanical problems. I would pass this car on to a Cameroonian student who had been admitted to pharmacy school and needed a car.

As I said, America isn't for the lazy or meek. You have to be smart and work hard to succeed. It has scammers, just like Third World nations. But what the American Dream delivers that other countries don't is FREEDOM. It is the reason most people migrate from Third World countries to the United States. Freedom of opportunity. Freedom to do the things that give value and bring joy to your life. The ability to take care of the things you can control, and let God take over which you have no control. Freedom to prioritize and balance the different aspects of your life. Simply put, as mentioned in our Declaration of Independence, the freedom to pursue your happiness. In most developing countries, people do not have as much freedom as in the US to plan their lives. Yes, people are happy in developing countries, but they are at the mercy of unstable governments, too much governmental control of their daily activities, and most importantly lack of opportunities.

How then do we pursue happiness in a place with so much freedom and, at the same time, so many distractions? We go back to the basics and simplify our lives. We rid our lives of all the clutter, which in the US happens to be material possessions, the things that have now become our American Dream. We get tempted daily to spend money on things that add no value to our lives. After reminding myself of my roots in Cameroon, living within my means suddenly became a life of luxury. The threshold for being thankful or showing my appreciation for the important things in my life is so much lower.

Thankfully, I married someone who had gone through similar

challenges. For example, when I got married, I already had a house that I had bought from a bank after it was repossessed from someone who couldn't afford it. It needed some work, but I was willing to live in one section and put in the time, with the help of some great construction guys, to remodel the house, just like we did in Africa. Before my wife moved in, after our wedding, the house was ready to be our first home. We had some credit card debt and school loans. When my friend Larry Allen, a bank president, sent us home to go take care of our debts, we took that to heart. We went home that day, listed all our debts, and embarked on a mission to pay them off. We were so serious that we picked up several overtime shifts to pay off the credit cards first. Second was the school loans, and then we tackled our car loans. My colleagues and friends thought we were crazy. We both had great paying jobs but needed extra money just to pay off debt. We didn't stop there. We decided to pay off our first home loan. Within three years, we were debt-free. By this time, we had our first son. We opened a 529 Student College Fund for him and started funding it. Then we rented out our first home which by this time was paid off. At the same time, we were capitalizing on our retirement accounts with our companies offering to match our retirement contributions. Then we bought our second home. All the money from the rent on the first house and one person's income went towards our emergency funds, children's college funds, vacations, paying down the second home, and most importantly, towards tithing and our mission work in Africa and Central America. As I write this, we are completely debt-free. Yes, including our homes. Our kids will have funding for college and beyond. We do not buy anything we can't afford. We save for our vacations before we go. We are not perfect, but we have a plan, and for now it's working.

Why is this important? Because for most immigrants the American Dream is this ridiculously delusional idea that we all unfortunately bought into. It is aggressively sold to us the moment we arrive. We start getting credit card offers in the mail. We are bombarded by TV commercials about the "dream car," or the "dream house," or the "zero-interest loans." Many of us fall into this trap and most will never be able to climb out of it. We compete with each other, show off our very expensive possessions that we don't own, and can't find peace because we must work to survive. We have become slaves of our own doing. Our new master is now money and debt. That's the trap of the American Dream that I caution new arrivals about.

Like I said, the American Dream is about FREEDOM, period. It is an enabler, for better and worse. Today, I work because I love what I do and my work allows me to make an even bigger contribution to my communities. It allows me to invest time and resources in the things that are most important to me.

Obviously, there are many ways to achieve your American Dream, and if you have peace of mind and happiness with your way, then please don't try to change a thing. If it works, why change it? However, always be ready to go back and re-evaluate your personal situation. If it's not working, then be flexible to make appropriate changes. Simplify your life and clear yourself of the worldly clutter that is preventing you from achieving your American Dream. Ask yourself, What is holding me back from my pursuit of happiness? What does it take to balance my life, so I can go back to focusing on what is important to me? How do I free myself from being enslaved by society's expectations of me or material possessions? Have a plan. Yogi Berra once said, "You've got to be very careful if you don't know where you're going, because you might not get there."

We all came to this country in search of freedom, prosperity and happiness. You have to ask yourself the tough question: What controls our hearts? What causes us to be anxious? What is keeping us from acquiring peace of mind? We have to make ourselves available to serve. Think about the first days of Jesus' discipleship. He went around calling on His first disciples to leave everything they had to follow Him. Today, if we got that same request, I am sure we would tell Him to wait a bit, so we could take care of the mortgage, the car payments and all our earthly obligations before we walk away with Him. America allows us to give more of ourselves and our resources to serve God. Don't get caught up in the materialism of our time. The true American Dream is within reach if you allow the freedoms of this country to work for you.

Three key events in my life changed the way I view money and material possessions. These all happened in West Texas. The first was a few months after I moved to West Texas. I was living paycheck to paycheck and struggling to make ends meet. In my second semester after paying my tuition, my checking account that I had opened in the Dallas area with a big national bank went negative. The bank charged me an overdraft fee and daily fees for having a negative balance. I visited the local branch of that bank on several occasions but was told that only the agent who opened the account could do anything to help me, so I had to visit the agent personally and explain the situation. The agent was in Fort Worth, over five hours away. She would not return my phone calls and I could not afford the time or money to drive to her bank.

My paycheck was being directly deposited to the bank. I couldn't close my account with a negative balance and I couldn't get my job to stop the direct deposit. All I could do was work harder to offset the daily fees and eventually get to positive. It took over three months for me to finally become positive, but I had lost a huge part of my monthly pay to bank fees. Once I got positive, I thought I could go see the manager one more time to plead for some refund.

When I got there, they kept me in the lobby for a long time, until finally the manager walked up to me and handed me a check for about ninety dollars. That was the positive balance on my account. She had decided to close my account and told me they didn't want my business. She wasn't interested in any explanations. I took the check to another national chain bank across town. That's when I was told that I had been reported to the ChexSystems, and I could not open an account with any bank. They gave me a number to call ChexSystems, and when I called, I was told that I had been reported by the big bank for writing hot checks. I tried to explain to them that I had never written a hot check. She apologized and said that only the bank could change that, and there was nothing she could do for me. All my attempts at opening an account with any other bank failed. Well, let's just say for almost one year I would have to go to work every other Friday to pick my check, then drive across town to one of the check cashing facilities that would charge me a certain percent to cash my check. I had to pay for everything in cash. I didn't have a credit card. This was extremely difficult, expensive and time consuming.

One day I decided to just walk into a small locally owned bank where I explained my case to them. They felt sorry for me and opened an account for me. I was able to get back on track with my direct deposit and finances. After this, I decided I would never bank with a major institution again. So, I stayed with the locally owned banks and still do to this day.

My second encounter with another locally-owned bank president is what I consider one on the most influential moments of my financial life. My wife and I were a young couple. I had been working as a physician assistant for over three years. We decided that we would live on my income, including paying down our debts and daily living expenses. She had just finished pharmacy school and was receiving a good income as well. Our plan was to invest her income in a project that would pay dividends, or the stock market. We reached out to Larry Allen, a local bank president. Larry had been to my clinic several times to talk to doctors about investments. We had met but never talked money. I called and made an appointment to see if he had investment ideas or opportunities for us. After looking at our finances, he asked us what our goals were. We responded that we wanted to be debt-free so that we could live life without the stress of debt. Larry looked at us and said that's not usually what he got from people. Most people just want to get rich. He told us that there are very few investments that would pay more than we were paying on credit cards, student loans and mortgage payments. So if our goal was to be debt-free, he advised us to go home and write down every single debt we had, then use my wife's salary to pay it off, while living strictly off my salary. After paying off our debts, then we could revisit the idea of investments and growing wealth. It was the best financial advice we ever received.

Larry's message was simple—live within your means. It was the first time anyone talked to me about wants and needs. I understood that there is a big difference between material things that we need and things that we want. Of course, you have to enjoy life, as most of my friends would tell me, but at what cost to you and your family's future? During this same time, my boss, realizing that I was different from most people in the way I approach finance and money, gave me a book he had read called *The Millionaire Next Door: The surprising secrets of America's Wealthy* by Thomas J. Stanley. When he handed the book to me he told me that he made many mistakes and didn't want me to fall prey to the same temptations. I read that book several times and passed it on to my wife. After reading the book, she and I took a vow to each other to keep our promise to become debt-free in ten years. It helped us with a destination. At this point we had to figure out how to get there.

We thought that as a bank president, Larry would have been happy to take our money and invest it in something that would make him and his bank more money. But he simply wanted to help us meet our goals and dream of being debt-free. Today, we owe no one, thanks to these two West Texas bank managers who took a little extra time to listen to us. We are free to invest our gifts as we pleased without the fear of going broke, something my wife and I still remember quite well.

There is a saying in Texas that "I wasn't born here, but I got here as fast as I could." I was not born in Lubbock, but I have successfully created a home in Lubbock. My dad wasn't born in the village of Munyenge but he successfully made Munyenge his home where he lived and raised his kids. Just like him, Lubbock has become my home because I am able to fulfill my dreams and can see hope in my children's future. West Texas not only embraced me, it allowed me the freedom to balance my time and to use my resources on the things that are important to me, including my faith, my family, and my friends. This is my American Dream.

Kyu Mee graduates from the Texas Tech School of Pharmacy.

Me with the infamous Mitsubishi Eclipse that I couldn't afford in Dallas.

CHAPTER 17

RACE RELATIONS

YOU ARE PROBABLY WONDERING why I would want to talk about race in America. It has become a polarizing and very controversial subject. People don't want to talk about it and if they do, it sometimes ends up in a fierce battle about who is right and who is wrong. I obviously have no academic qualifications to give comments on such a controversial topic. However, I do believe that my experience has offered me a very unique perspective into race relations in the US.

The way I view race has been crucial in defining who I am today. I write to encourage, and hopefully to inspire, an honest conversation about this topic. At least I write for my two boys, Zigo and Zi Chan, who may find these observations useful someday.

I suspect that most people born in America have had some sort of conversation or encounter about race. For some, it is with a family member; for others, in school or a public encounter. Whatever the case, we start building our understanding of others at a very young age. Most people, black or white, will eventually develop an opinion about race based on their experiences.

Prior to arriving in the United States, I had never lived with anyone from a different race. I once asked my father about slavery, after learning about it in school, and he told me that all he remembered were stories about "white men" coming to the villages with gifts, and then taking back with them young strong African men and women with the offer to teach them modern civilization and special skills, including how to fight their enemies. Those young people never returned. My father had advised me not to worry about being taken away, because it didn't happen anymore. He did tell me about another country in Africa where people were still fighting for freedom, and about Nelson Mandela.

I was somewhat curious about what it was like to grow up being black in a country like South Africa. How could anyone ever forgive after such brutal treatment of Africans by European transplants? So, in coming to America, I never thought I would find myself in a country where all races lived together and had to openly and equitably deal with the challenges of race relations.

I came to the US during a racially charged period—in the midst of the O.J. Simpson murder trial. I had never heard his name prior to arriving on the campus of my private Christian university in Arkansas. My university was predominantly white, with probably well below 5 percent black Americans, and fewer than 100 Africans like myself. Because it was a Christian university, most of my friends' parents were pastors in Arkansas and other communities mostly in Southern states such as Tennessee, Louisiana, Alabama, Mississippi and Texas. In my opinion, I would say the university did a great job in not only integrating black students but also in making everyone feel at home.

The university would pair students of different races as roommates. Since I didn't have a preference, they paired me with a white roommate. I enjoyed a great relationship with all races. I was naturally drawn to the black American students because they were racially familiar to me and reminded me of my friends in Africa. I was equally drawn to the white population because all I knew of Caucasians was how they brought sustainable healthcare and education to my ancestral village in Cameroon, and I was a beneficiary of their acts of love.

To us villagers, white was white. We didn't differentiate a white person from Europe from someone from Australia or America. Everyone was white, and for all I knew they could have been from the same country. But what was striking was how different my interactions with the different groups were. American Caucasians were very curious about me and my country. They asked questions about my family, village life, education and day-to-day living. The image they had of Africa was more of an intriguing or exotic place to vacation rather than an impoverished Third World continent. Black Americans, on the other hand, asked questions more about the social life and were curious what it was like to live in a place with just one race. There was little interest in wanting to go visit. For some reason, I expected the black Americans to be more curious about Africa, as this was their ancestral home.

As time went on, despite the friendliness of the student body, I also noticed an underlying separation between the two, especially in the dormitories and the cafeteria. The black students tended to hang out with other students of the same race, as did the white students. When we hung out all together, there were rarely any conversations about race, but when I spent time alone with the different races, people spoke very freely about racial issues. Even the white students would speak to me almost as if they didn't notice I was black. Sometimes, after having a conversation with one group, I would bring it up with the other group, and I would be cautioned for it. At times, it felt like I was cheating on a friend.

Things became even more confusing to me as the O.J. Simpson trial got close to a verdict. The students were getting increasingly segregated. One day I asked my white roommate to explain to me what was going on. His answer was simple: a black man killed a white woman and was trying to get away with it. That same day, I went to visit one of my black American friends in his room. There were several black students talking about the case, but their opinion was quite different. O.J Simpson was innocent, and the white police officers were trying to pin it on him because he was a successful black man. When I got back to the room, my white roommate wanted to know what the black kids thought about the case. He seemed to fear that I would be corrupted by their point of view.

On the day of the verdict, we had the usual morning church service. The school president talked about the trial and called for peace and calm on campus. He said whatever the verdict was, he expected everyone to respect it and go on with his or her life. We held hands and prayed together for the country and the families of the victims. We were asked to go back to our dormitories and stay inside. As we walked out of the auditorium I was fearful that something bad might happen. The crowd got increasingly segregated the farther we walked to the dormitories; I found myself walking alone. I didn't know where to go. I pondered what side I would join in the event of a riot or fight. None of it made sense to me.

I went to my dorm as instructed and stayed there, not knowing what was going to happen. My roommate walked in, complaining that O.J. had hired bunch of good lawyers to help him walk free. I asked him that if it was a certainty that O.J. killed his wife, why was there a need for a trial. He didn't understand, so I explained to him that in my country, especially in the village, if you are accused of killing someone, especially if there was an eyewitness, or if proved by the village witch doctor, you would be lucky if the police found you before the village vigilantes did.

After the verdict, I could tell there were small segregated groups standing around venting. The teachers and campus police officers walked through the dormitories making sure everyone was okay and even offering counseling to students. Thankfully, everything went back to normal without any incidents on campus. However, I would be left with more questions than answers. Out of this experience, one thing I knew was that as an African, I was treated differently by the white schoolmates partly because I did not have the defensive shield that some black Americans have developed over time from centuries of racism. I was considered "safe" to talk to about racial issues. I was often invited to the homes of white students to meet their families or friends, which was not the case for most black Americans on campus.

You have to realize that by 1995, I had faced class discrimination in Africa but never racial discrimination. I despised class discrimination, but I had come to terms with the fact that I was poor, a farmer's son, and to some seemed primitive because of my lack of sophistication. But all those things I could change, which gave me a sense of hope. If you're hated because of your skin color, there isn't much you can do about that.

The first time I personally experienced a hateful racial act against me was in Arkansas. I needed some school supplies and had asked a friend to drop me off at a nearby retail store. I planned to walk back to school. As I crossed the parking lot to get to the main road leading to school, I heard someone say something. I wasn't sure if they were talking to me. As I turned around, I saw a white middle-aged man who angrily screamed the N-word at me and asked what I was doing there. I had never heard that word before, and I wasn't sure what he was saying.

With an apologetic smile, I told him that I was sorry. I was just trying to cross the road to get back to school. Upon hearing my accent, his facial expression immediately changed. He stopped walking and asked me where I was from. I said Africa. He asked if I was a student at the university. Then, with a genuine smile, he said, "Welcome to America, glad to have you here." He then offered me a ride to my dormitory.

In the car he apologized for calling me the N-word and tried to explain that some black kids had been causing trouble in the area. He was happy that I wasn't one of them. That evening, my roommate explained to me what that word meant. Knowing his explanation wasn't as descriptive—or offensive—as what my black friends would likely tell me, I decided to research the word on my own. I found out it was considered the most offensive word in the English language. So why would someone who didn't even know me call me that?

To this day, I run into someone at least once a month curious about my accent and origins. They often say the same thing me: "Welcome to America, glad to have you here." Often it is from my patients who seem genuinely happy to have me. The first person to welcome me to the US was the pilot upon landing at the Atlanta airport in 1995. Every month I am reminded by this simple phrase of acknowledgement and appreciation how truly blessed I am to be in a place where I am welcome. It is a phrase that recharges my batteries. It always feels refreshing to know that, regardless of what I am going through, someone is glad I am here.

I have two sons who were born in the US. They will never get that "welcoming" remark because they were born-here African Americans. This is their home. The stories most black Americans have heard are that their ancestors were brought here against their will, that they didn't freely come here like I did. On the other hand, my white American friends tell me that they feel they are being blamed for the sins of their ancestors. One thing I know is that everyone wants to move on and raise their children in a place that is peaceful, loving and free, but we are being held back by our past and our unwillingness to have an honest and respectful conversation on how race affects our society. We are held back by our preconceptions. Including me.

One evening a few years ago, I was vacationing with some friends. After dinner, we sat around the kitchen counter talking about mission work and Africa. Everyone there was a physician except me, and we had all known each other a long time. One of the friends, a female African, jokingly asked the other friend, a female black American, why black Americans in general are not interested in Africa. The African woman is from Cameroon and had been to Cameroon with me on a mission trip. She suggested that not many black Americans go on mission trips or show interest in visiting Africa. She, too, had expected black Americans to be more interested in Africa when she came to the US. The black American woman who was married to an African man had somewhat of an emotional response: she grew up in Alabama and her mother was one of the first black kids to be integrated into white schools in the 1960s. She started by telling us that she has always been curious about her heritage and indeed had recently done a DNA test which showed that she was 32 percent Nigerian, 28 percent Ivory Coast, 11 percent Cameroonian, 8 percent European, and 3 percent Asian. Now that she has this information, where does she go next? She had more questions than answers.

She elaborated that most black Americans do have a culture, the African-American culture. It is their relationship to their families, where they live, their churches and immediate family background, rather than the distant past that they don't have any connection to anymore. She went on to say that the likelihood of most African Americans being able to go to Africa is so slim because they're poor. She mentioned to us that, as a physician in Texas, she still supports her local church in Alabama, and it is probably the reason the church can keep the lights on. Most of the kids can't even imagine leaving their state, let alone going out of the country and across the world.

The other issue: There is widespread poverty among blacks in America. So why go to another country to help impoverished blacks?

When I moved to Texas, Uncle Francis warned that I would face racism, but he also coached me not to let it define who I was, or how I treated the next person. He taught me that even the most racist person deserves redemption and I must never forget that I may be the one to plant that seed of enlightenment. He warned me that if I let a racial act define me, I would build a defensive wall between me and others that would prevent me from reaching my full potential in this country.

Through the years, I have truly been blessed with friends from all races. I now understand that part of this is because of my preconception or lack of it about race, and the other part is my basic belief about the need to be rid us of our prejudices and respect each other as created in God's image.

Nelson Mandela once said, "No one is born hating another person because of the color of their skin or his background or religion. People must learn to hate, and if they can learn to hate they can be taught to love, for love comes more naturally to the human heart than the opposite." Knowing that Nelson Mandela was able to forgive the people who imprisoned him for twenty-seven years helped me understand that he was calling on us all to preach love to our kids, friends, neighbors and enemies. But before we can do this, we must accept the truth about racism in America, and listen and understand how it affects a society, and open our hearts to reconciliation.

My mixed-race sons deserve to know the truth. They are growing up in one of the most racially diverse nations on earth, while I grew up in a place with no diversity. There will be people who will treat them differently because of the color of their skin. They are going to face prejudice and it could come from any race. Our job as parents is to teach them how to overcome these challenges, like uncle Francis did to me, and show them how to love like I have experienced in the people I today call friends.

One Saturday morning, I woke up early to work on my yard. I mowed the lawn, cleared the grass and trimmed the trees. I would occasionally go out behind the house to put my trash in the dumpster. On one of my trips walking back from the alley, I ran into one of the neighbors from a different street. I said good morning and she responded and we went our separate ways. A few hours later, after my yard work, I decided to drive to our mission storage unit to arrange some medical supplies. On my way out of the neighborhood, I saw an estate sale sign, so I decided to see if they had anything for sale that we might need. I took a tour of the items and decided I didn't need anything there. On my way out, there was a table by the door hosted by three ladies. The lady in the middle, whom I assumed was the house owner, asked if she had just seen me in the alley that morning. I responded yes, and without skipping a beat, her friend asked if I was going through the dumpster and if I found anything that I wanted. Realizing what had just happened, the homeowner jumped up, was very embarrassed and apologized to me. She then told the friend that I was the new athletic coach that had just moved into the neighborhood. On my way out, I could hear her scolding her friend for embarrassing her. I thought about this and could only conclude that the friend could not see how someone like me could afford a house in that neighborhood. If I am in the alley, then I must be going through someone's trash.

I posted the incident on my Facebook page. Within seconds, I received numerous comments from people who have faced this same situation. After the first few comments, I posted that I was not interested in angry or hateful comments, but think that we need to have a dialogue and accept the fact that these prejudices still exist. The only way we can create a better future for our children is to be comfortable talking about it. I received comments from Hispanics, Asians, Middle Easterners, blacks and gays who all used this as a forum to say similar things have happened to them, but more importantly suggested that dialogue was the only way we can begin the road to reconciliation.

The most impressionable Facebook comments were from

my white friends who were all shocked that something like that had happened to me. Some offered to go find this person and tell them who I was. Some suggested that these people must have bad parents. Now what is important here is that, in no part of the posting did I mention that the woman who made the comment was white. If you go back and look at my descriptions you will agree that the woman could easily be black, Hispanic or any other race.

Because of our preconceptions and prejudices, we have deprived ourselves of the incredibly rich resources that every culture has to offer. If you watch cable news these days, most of what we see about race is people arguing about who is right and who is wrong. Who has the better argument? People talking over each other for their time to shine on television. It seems no answers to the problems are presented, just analysis on who, what, why. It seems that they are always trying to find problems with every situation. Two years ago, my wife and I decided to cancel our twenty-four-hour news channels because we felt that our kids deserve to see adults having disagreements in a civil manner. It's what we as adults teach them—to be constructive and be good listeners.

While writing this section of the book, I was sitting in a tire shop waiting for my flat to be fixed. It was a few days after the Trayvon Martin case. A gentleman walked in, not seeing me, and started a conversation with the front desk clerk about the case. The customer informed the clerk that the shooter, Zimmerman, was not guilty, so the news media should let the case go. He went on to say, you know these black kids, he was probably at the wrong place and at the wrong time and got what he deserved.

I didn't know the details of the case, but couldn't help but ask myself whether being shot and killed is just punishment for being at the wrong place. As the father of two sons who will someday be somewhere they're not supposed to be, I can only pray that they don't run into someone like this customer. We may never know if Martin's death was racially motivated, but at the end of the day, a family had just lost their son. We have become so desensitized that we can have a casual conversation about the justifiable reasons for killing another person.

So, how do we start this dialogue? First, we have to accept the facts and realities of race discrimination in America.

1. Slavery and slave trading did exist where people were considered less than human and sold to the highest bidder.
2. If someone is discriminated against solely because of the color of his or her skin, they feel angry and usually don't forget this event.
3. When anyone is accused of being racist towards another race and that wasn't their intention, they feel angry and usually don't forget.
4. Most people who are discriminated against or accused of racism usually develop protective psychological barriers against the other race, especially if the accused is innocent.

These acknowledgments can be achieved through education. During my first two years of college, I took several classes that touched on the topic of slavery in the US, but it was talked about as a historical fact, which has no relevance to today's America. I learned more about slave trade and slavery as a twelve-year-old kid in Africa than I did in all my classes here. So, I wasn't surprised to find out that few of my classmates knew anything about the significance of slavery in the building of this country. It's something that occurred and was very important in most decision making at the highest levels of the United States government in shaping this country into what it is today. If our children are not taught these facts in schools, they will eventually learn from other sources that may not have the facts right, and may approach it from a biased standpoint. This applies to all the races.

We must teach the good and the bad just as we do when we teach about the wars and other major events in our early years. Obviously, there is nothing good about slavery. However, the country learned a lot about itself through the fight to abolish slavery, and out of that process we got great leaders who taught us about forgiveness, the need to not compromise our right of freedom and speech. In other countries, especially African countries, you dare not talk about your rights or criticize the government.

Once we all agree on these facts, then we have to figure out how to reconcile. The first thing we must do is be open to listen to others on how racial acts threaten the dignity of another human being. Then we have to understand that everyone deserves that basic right to fulfill his or her best potential. Finally, we must be willing to forgive each other.

During the Sermon on the Mount, Jesus gives us what we Christians called the Lord's Prayer. Central to every one of us is when He said "forgive us our sins as we forgive everyone who trespasses against us" and "deliver us from evil." The things I have been through certainly do not compare with more atrocities like the Texas dragging death of the African American man, nor do I claim to understand what everyone feels, but I know that my ability to forgive has released me from the prison of anger and revenge. Such release would allow us to drop the protective shield of guilt and accusations, and allow people access to enrich our lives. A future free from discrimination starts from these basic principles and a hope for a better tomorrow for our children. Don't underestimate the power of forgiveness. There are people who truly will never meet their full potential because, due to preconceptions or prejudices, they are unable to befriend someone of a different race.

I met a young guy at a barbershop during my first years in the Dallas-Fort Worth area who, after finding out I was a nurse's aide, informed me that he would rather be homeless than work in a nursing home to wipe a white man's butt. He told me that only Africans do that type of job because it was created to keep us inferior. He did not have a job and was living with his mother, and he went to the barbershop during the day to pass time. I wondered where he learned something like that. I know that this job was what exposed me to the medical field and got me where I am today. I also understand that if I had been born in the US, with daily occurrences of discrimination, I might have had the same ideas as he.

In my years in the US, I have been exposed to many black kids like this young man. Some I have reached out to in an attempt to inspire them. I usually tell them about my background and, as an African in America, failure is not an option for me. I tell them that being born in America, regardless of their circumstances, still puts them ahead of many young people around the world. Some I have been able to influence, but some of these young kids often return to the same place, which usually portrays them as victims with the unintended consequences of making them believe that success from their surroundings is an impossible uphill climb.

Yes, I have been in situations where people get up and walk away when you approach them. I have been in situations where people grab their purses tighter when I walk close. I have even been in situations where people have asked me to go back to Africa where I came from. However, the overwhelming response I have received is people opening their hearts to me. People in small towns, especially in West Texas, have gone out of their way to make me feel welcomed. Which one of these reactions do I choose to be influenced by? I make the decision to go with the latter because it's done with love, and love will always triumph over hate, as it comes more naturally.

I was back at a black barbershop one day, just as school was letting out. Several kids, including my barber's son, were hanging out at the shop while I was getting my haircut. The barbers and adults in the room were having a conversation about racism at their school. The son had a bad grade and another's son was not getting enough playing time on the football team. They were talking about how racism at the school was to blame for their failures.

I could see the kids listening in approval. After I finished my cut, I asked to talk to the dad. I explained to him that having this conversation so casually in the presence of the kids was detrimental to them. I explained in my own simple terms that my father would never let me get away with that. By telling the kids that they were failing because of the color of their skin, a fact they could never change, we gave them permission to fail. We had just given them a reason for not wanting to work harder.

As we talked, the man said he "never thought about it that way." He agreed with me and very much appreciated the conversation.

The next time I was there I found out that he had shared our conversation with the rest of the fathers. He even had a magazine containing an article that had been written about me on display.

I have had people attempt to assure me that they are not racist, by telling me that they don't see color, and that when they see me they don't see black, or they don't want to see black. I explain to them that I want them to see the black in me. That is who I am. I am black, and I am from Africa. That is my heritage. That is my story. If you don't see that in me, then you don't see me. You are then missing out on a very important part of me. This is what God made me to look like. It is how I was packaged to be introduced into the world. It is the color of that gift wrapping. He did it for a reason, and I can just hope that I am using it for that purpose. When I tell young kids, especially black kids, my story, I want them to be inspired. I want them to see that if a young black kid from a remote farming village in Africa can do it, they can too.

I coached one of my four-year-old son's soccer teams. During one of our first practices, one of his teammates asked if they could touch my hair. His mother was a little embarrassed, but I was excited. The kid was just being curious. It was my little chance to break that cycle of fear of offending the other race. Not only did I let him touch my hair, I gave the other kids the opportunity to touch my hair and my skin if they wanted. The kid's response on touching my hair was, "That is so cool." I knew that if I had said no, most likely the kid's mother would have given him a lecture about not asking black people to touch their hair. I am sure everyone feels different about my reaction. However, this is an example of how we start building racial barriers at a very young age. We need to break the cycle.

With Kyu Mee, my wife, and our two boys, Zigo (left) and Zi Chan (right).

CHAPTER 18

PARENTING

BY NOW YOU KNOW that I enjoyed a very special relationship with my father. I am going to contrast my father's parenting ways with what I have come to understand as good parenting in the US.

I had spent seven years practicing pediatric neurosurgery in a very busy trauma center in West Texas. Every time we are consulted, part of my examination is to evaluate for potential child abuse. On a few occasions, I have had to call child protective services. Typically, this is done when you find evidence of physical abuse. We do this because we as medical providers have to advocate for the patient/child and also to catch a problem before the situation gets worse. Based on the criteria that I have used in my practice to evaluate for potential abuse, I can say that if these same standards were used in my village, all our parents would be in jail. On the other hand, if my dad were to spend a day with me as a parent, he would probably be disappointed in my parenting skills. I can picture him shaking his head saying, "That's not how I raised you."

Growing up, none of us children had any doubt how much our parents loved and cared about us, especially after a spanking. Our relationship was great because that was a father-son relationship at its best in that part of the world. It was never a friendship. The father talks, the child listens. The father instructs, the child obeys. If my parents spoke to me in the dialect, then I respond in the dialect. Our parents never learned English and so we were not to speak to them in a language that they hadn't learned. This was considered extremely disrespectful. This is one of the reasons we ended up learning multiple languages.

Our parents spoke our ancestral dialect and the common Pidgin English, and when addressing them we were expected to as well. It was understood that your parents were not your friends. I played soccer through primary school, secondary, and high school, but my father never came to watch my games. Now, I can picture some of you reading saying, "Aw, that's so sad." It's not. My father did not like soccer and never wanted to encourage the activity. He saw many kids abandon their education with hopes of becoming professional soccer players. Time and time again, none of them ever made it. Kids would leave the village with high aspirations and returned deflated, settling back in as village farmers. To the parents in my village, education was the ticket out of the hard manual labor, disease, corruption and despair. Dad told us that we were wasting our time on something that wouldn't get us anywhere. I knew he was proud of me because he told his friends, and I saw it on his face when people would stop by the house to congratulate me on a performance.

There was an understanding by all the parents that if any one of them saw a child doing something wrong, the other parent had permission to discipline that child and then make sure to report the incident to the child's parents. Sometimes you might get an additional spanking if the offense was very serious. Like every child, I thought our parents overreacted, but we never got angry, at least never in their presence. We would hold our anger or frustration until they were out of sight.

My father was a tough guy to please, and because of that we worked extremely hard to impress him. I worked the hardest. I am sure some of my sisters would dispute this. This is because they, too, fell victim to the blunt end of my father's cane. Much of that was my fault. My father was tougher on my sisters, especially when it was a *"boy palava,"* something that had to do with boys. Dating was an absolute no in our household. You dated when you got married. Father made it very clear that if any one of the girls got pregnant, he was going to disown her and remove her from school.

Everyone in our village knew that my father had a gun and wasn't afraid to use it to protect his girls. On one occasion, he intercepted a handwritten message from a boy proposing a rendezvous with one of my sisters behind a famous big boma tree. My father went there early and waited for him to show up. When the boy arrived, he gave him a few swats and showed him his gun, telling him to go tell all the boys in the village that the next time it would not be a cane. This is how my father got the nickname *Idi Amin Dada.* The village boys truly believed that he wasn't afraid to take their lives if they messed with his daughters.

My sisters for years wondered how my father managed to know everything. Well, a few years ago I confessed that I was his spy and informant. I was part of a small group of mischievous nine-year-old rascals who knew everything that was going on in our village. Since all of us children slept in the same room, I would pretend to be asleep and would listen in on my sisters' boy gossip. I was the only boy in a house full of girls for many years, so the village boys usually bribed me with candy and money to take notes to my sisters. Little did they know that I could read. I would open the notes, read them out to my dad, eat their candy and keep their money, and then take the notes to my sisters. As much as we loved each other, we competed as to who was going the get the other in more trouble. Me against the girls. Today my sisters laugh at me when I try to teach my boys not to snitch on each other. Though I rarely got in trouble, when I did it was usually quite serious, and my sisters loved it.

My most grievous offense was when I stole some mangos from a neighbor's farm. Our neighbor had a mango tree that produced the sweetest mangos. His mangos were mostly transported out of the village to be sold in the city. One day, two of my friends convinced me to go to his farm and steal the mangos. I was feeling quite adventurous that day. Not only did

I go with them, I also volunteered to climb the large mango tree and let them stay on the ground and pick up the mangos as I harvested and threw them on the forest floor. All of a sudden, I realized no one was collecting and counting them. When I called out, I knew something was wrong as my friends had all disappeared. Then I heard the owner chasing them in the forest. I hurriedly climbed down the tree, but unfortunately the farmer spotted me and called out my name. My friends and I regrouped a little later and decided that we were going to lie all the way to our graves that it wasn't us. Theft was one of the most grievous offenses in the village. Our parents could never find out.

My case was worse because this would be my second offense in a week. A few days prior, I had taken a pencil from one of my classmates without his permission. I lost it, and since I couldn't afford to replace it, I said I hadn't taken it. His father was the church catechist (deacon) who managed the kids' Bible study class. Knowing quite well from my classmate that I took the pencil, his dad spent that entire week teaching us about the Ten Commandments and how people who steal burn for eternity. I knew he was directing the sermon at me, at least that's how I felt. Finally, I confessed. The image of burning in hell with no one to bring me water to quench my thirst was too much for me to handle.

My friends used this against me. I promised that I would not confess this time, regardless. We took a solemn oath to each other and went our separate ways. That evening, the mango grower came to visit my dad. I had rehearsed my lines, facial expression and posture. I blatantly lied to my dad. This time I wouldn't go free. He was too smart for me. He asked me to take off my shirt. He pulled me towards him, examined my belly and sent my sisters to go get his whipping cane and the Bible. Knowing that he had caught me, I started crying and asking for forgiveness. On my belly was clear evidence that I had climbed a tree that day. I had fresh scratches from hugging the mango tree as I climbed. Worse, he knew it was a mango tree because the sap was still on my belly and he not only could see the streaks, he could smell the distinct scent of mango sap. Needless to say, I received a beating, not a spanking, a beating for committing four major sins against the Ten Commandments. My dad handed me the Bible and asked me to name the sins I had committed. Lying, stealing, and coveting my neighbor's property was easy to find, but the sin that was most important to my dad was more elusive. With tears obstructing my view, I managed to find the last sin: dishonoring my father.

I was about nine years old, and I can't remember ever again taking another person's property without their permission. And if it crossed my mind, I could hear my father's voice from above my shoulders quietly narrating the commandments to me. The point of this story is that bad parenting in my village was letting the children off without "proper" punishment for their crimes. For my parents, punishment was spankings. They took "spare the rod, and spoil the child" approach to a whole new level.

I recently asked my mother about this form of parenting. Her response was that we grew up in a place with no second chances. They were so worried about kids going astray and ending up ruining their lives. She was particularly worried about peer pressure. We were never allowed to date, we couldn't leave the house after dark unless it was a church or school-related event, and even then we had to be accompanied by an adult family member. And by the way, adult is not age eighteen, it's when your parents say you are an adult. For most of our parents, that means after marriage. They worried about us contracting diseases that had no cure such as HIV, or getting caught in drug dealing or usage, or going to jail for being accused of a crime.

When you were accused of a crime in my village, and you didn't have the money to bribe the police, which most of our parents didn't, you went to jail. Once in jail, you were at the mercy of a very corrupt system. My parents were strict in order to protect us.

I have come full circle. My wife, Kyu Mee, and I are raising our two beautiful boys in a society that couldn't be more different than where we were both born. However, we will face similar fears and challenges as we try to balance discipline and building a solid relationship for them. Contrary to my dad, I strive to build a friendly relationship with my boys to enable them to have an open communication with me. In a society where they will be faced with many options as they get older, I want to make sure that they feel confident in my ability to protect them, care for them, and provide for them just like I felt with my father. I can't help, however, asking myself what my dad would say if he saw my kids wasting food, wanting something different than what is presented to them on the dinner table, or watching me negotiate and compromise with them. That was never the case with my father's family.

With myself and Kyu Mee, our time as a family with our children is most precious. I have a hard time going a day without seeing them. I am heavily involved in their activities, especially soccer. It is the one sport, in a country with plenty of options, where I can pass my skills on to them. For my father, this was farming. We sit down for dinner as a family and talk about my children's day, just like my father did with his children. I read to them every night and wish my father had been able to read to me. In my own way, I want them to understand that I am just their caretaker and their true father is God. He just picked me because He knows I would be the perfect person to help them find their purpose.

It's a different way of parenting, but in the end, like my parents, I believe that we are their initial window to the world. I must give them the tools to not only succeed in life but to find their God-given purpose on this earth, and to seize every opportunity to help others find theirs. I know that they will grow to understand the world around them, based on what we have taught them. Above all, through us they should understand that God created them in His image and for His purpose.

My children will never endure the hardship my father went through, nor will they experience the financial hardships I endured. But they won't take life for granted, either. For now, they have me to lean on for support, but there will come a time when these lessons will be all they have to sustain them. I will have to teach them to preserve their personal dignity and protect their basic right to freedom that this great country has afforded us.

Coaching my boys' soccer teams.

Hanging out with Dad during a break from the clinic on our second mission trip.

My sons, incubating eggs for their poultry.

My boys take care of their chickens and collecting eggs.

My mother taught my son
how to water plants.

My son, Zigo, on his first visit to my village of Munyenge.

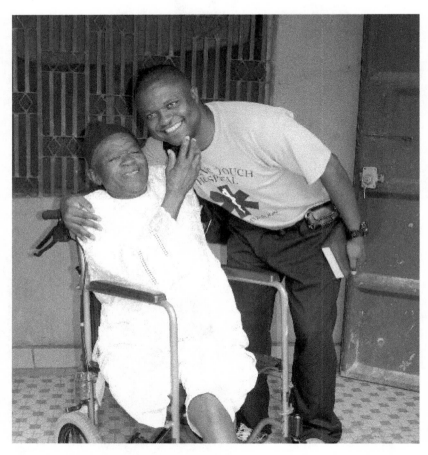

With my father on our second mission trip to Cameroon.

With my first son, Zigo.

With my mother (middle) and sisters in Lubbock.

With my mother.

With my second son, Zi Chan

With my sons, Zigo and Zi Chan.

With my wife, Kyu Mee, and our two boys, Zigo and Zi Chan.

Zigo gets his little brother ready for a family wedding.

CHAPTER 19

FAMILY LEGACY

IN HIS INAUGURAL ADDRESS on January 20th, 1961, President Kennedy told the American people to "Ask not what your country can do for you—ask what you can do for your country." I learned this phrase in secondary school during our American History class. As I previously said, one of my favorite American presidents was JFK. Maybe it was because his brother was murdered, too. Or it could be that he worked to fight for African-American rights.

My interest in Kennedy's life and policies started when I was just a young boy in Cameroon, before I ever knew about his political affiliations. So, it was not the politics. I believe it was the way it was presented to us by my secondary school teacher. I do know that reading about him introduced me to something unique about Americans: their incredible generosity to other countries and people in need. My teacher told us that America was the most powerful nation on earth. In my little fourteen-year-old brain, all I could think was in terms of might, that there is God and then there is the United States. A country that powerful should not need anything from anyone. They have the money to get anything they wanted.

Why would a president be talking about people doing things for the country? Why does he spend a lot of time talking about helping the poor? He said, "To those people in the huts and villages of half the globe struggling to break the bonds of misery, we pledge our best efforts to help them help themselves, for whatever period is required—not because the communists may be doing it, not because we seek their votes, but because it is right. If a free society cannot help the many who are poor, it cannot save the few who are rich." I memorized that speech because I thought the teacher might call on me to present it in front of my class. I did not understand much of it until I came to the US.

Up to that time in my life, the only exposures I had to people in positions of power were government officials who would frequently visit my village, and during my first year of secondary school in Sasse. So far, it hadn't been positive. The whole idea of a country protecting its citizens or the rich caring for the poor was almost nonexistent, except in the context of the church or the villagers helping each other, but not a government official going out of their way to help you. My experience in the US has been different. The first thing that was shocking to me was when people would say that they elected an official who represented and worked for them. They could always elect other people if their officials were not doing their jobs. This concept was most foreign to me. Almost every official I had met was appointed—not elected. In my years in the US, I had heard and met people who had been helped by the government and by officials using their position of power to influence positive change to help others. Little did I know that I would one day need the assistance of some of the highest-ranking officials in the US government.

Coming from a country where the diagnosis of cancer mostly ends up poorly, my mother would get a second chance at life. She is a living testimony of how far an act of generosity can go. An act that would quite literally reinforce my belief in the goodness of mankind and that call to action by JFK.

I haven't spoken much about my mother in this book because her purpose and her story are still being accomplished. Before my dad's passing, my mother had been by his side every step of the way, especially during the last seven years of his life after his amputation. The sixty-plus year monogamous relationship between my parents in a polygamous era deserves an entire book of its own. However, I couldn't talk about American generosity without telling you how miracles do happen.

My mother, Josephine, has a heart of gold. Her entire life has been dedicated to serving others, and sometimes at the risk of neglecting her own health. She has eight biological children and over twenty other children whom she raised; we all call her "Mother." As of this writing, she continues to raise many other children in her home. It was not uncommon for my mom, after traveling to visit friends or family members, to come back home with a child. We always knew that if the new addition was introduced to us as a brother or sister, it meant they had come to stay. If it was a cousin or some other introduction, then we knew it was a temporary arrangement, but it typically converted to permanent. It didn't matter to us. We had a big farm that could feed an entire school if needed. No one was ever turned away from the house.

Once a new kid arrived, your position in the family changed. That could mean you had to adjust to sleeping with one more person in your bed. We had two beds in our room—one for the boys and one for the girls. We slept crosswise to fit more people on the bed.

Mom was known by the villagers as the woman who could not walk past a hungry child without bringing him or her home or helping them attend school. Several times Mother would go to Fontem to visit her parents, and return with another mouth to feed. My many brothers and sisters still today consider ourselves siblings, and we are bound by the common feeling that our mother made us feel like the most fortunate kids on earth. She would tell me that her most important but challenging job was taking care of my father after his amputation. In his last years of life, Father was so arthritic from farm work that he needed help with personal hygiene, sitting and even transferring in and out of his wheelchair. Mom was his nurse and an incredible one. She did everything for him, including administering his insulin shots.

After our clinic was opened, she and Father would go to the hospital in Muyuka religiously for their annual checkups.

She would call me with the results. Kathy Marcum had visited Muyuka so frequently that many patients, including my parents, considered her their personal physician. They insisted on calling her "Doctor" Kathy, though she is a PA. Because of this relationship, Mother was willing to tell Dr. Kathy details about her personal health. Traditional mothers don't tell their sons anything about gynecological health and we don't ask any questions. It's just out of respect.

One day in 2012, I called Cameroon to check on the family. We had our typical conversations with Mom and Dad, which usually ended with them going down the list, asking about all my friends that they had met during the mission trips. When we got to Dr. Kathy, Mom said she wanted me to tell her that she was having some persistent vaginal bleeding. She said it wasn't urgent, that she would wait until she was able to see Dr. Kathy on the next trip. Mother assured me not to worry as she was not in pain. I asked her a few more questions and immediately became concerned. She had lost some weight, reported generalized weakness and loss of appetite. I got off the phone with her and immediately called our resident physician at Healing Touch Hospital. I advised mother to immediately go down for a checkup to the following day.

I am not a gynecologist, but I recalled that one of the things they drilled into us during my training was that painless vaginal bleeding in a postmenopausal woman is cancer until proven otherwise. My mother did not know this. To her it was just bleeding, which is common to all women. The next day I received a call from the doctor, who confirmed my biggest fear. On his examination he saw what he suspected was cervical cancer, which was actively bleeding and had invaded the surrounding tissue. Without any radiologic capability or means to do a biopsy, he would have to send Mother to the city of Douala for testing.

Through my mother's ordeal, I started getting a glimpse of truly how bad the medical situation in Cameroon was. I called every doctor I knew for help. I was told that there were only two functional CAT scan machines in the entire country, one in Douala, the economic capital, and one in Yaounde, the capital of the country. It would take at least a week, even if I had extra money to pay the workers and the doctors to get her to the top of the list. While waiting to get the CAT scan, we sent her for a biopsy. A few days later the results came in. My mother had endometrial adenocarcinoma, a malignant form of uterine cancer. She was immediately admitted to the hospital to treat her anemia. The gynecologist also informed me that the pathology results suggested that the uterine cancer had invaded the cervix. When I called my sister in Boston, who is a nurse, to tell her the bad news, she reminded me that it couldn't be true because my mother previously had a complete hysterectomy by one of the best doctors in Cameroon seven years prior to her symptoms. It was a confusing time for us. We really needed a CAT scan.

After visiting with a few colleagues in the US, we decided to get my mother to the States for treatment. My mother had lost faith in the medical care she was getting. She understood her prognosis as told to her and my sister by the best cancer doctor in Cameroon. She requested to be taken back home so that she could die by her husband and children. My mother's biggest fear was dying away from home. She also wanted to make sure that things were in order at home and to make plans for my father's care in her absence.

I started contacting local US doctors and hospitals with the results of her tests to find out the cost of further studies, possible surgical intervention and radiation. Once I got some pricing, I then contacted the US Embassy in Cameroon to inquire about requirements for a medical visa to the US. They wanted proof that she was indeed my mother, as well as the exact anticipated cost of travel and treatment, and proof that my wife and I could afford such treatment. They also needed letters from accepting doctors and hospitals. I gathered all the documents and made Mom an appointment with the embassy. We made all necessary arrangements, and bought her flight ticket to travel back with my sister. Two days before the interview, she would again reluctantly embark on the two-day journey from the village to the capital city, Yaounde, where the embassy is located.

In the US, we were anxiously waiting. I received a call informing me that the embassy had denied her a travel visa. After reviewing all the documents, they felt that we could not afford cancer treatment in the US and that my mother would be a burden on American society. I spoke to my mom who adamantly informed me that she was at peace with the decision to remain in her village. She told me that God probably didn't want her to die away from home or burden us with trying to get her body back to Cameroon. I was devastated. I begged my mother not to give up on us. I began the appeal process with the US embassy but was again denied a medical visa. I got off the phone, stayed in my office and cried like a baby.

The chief medical officer, Dr. Randy Hickle, walked in to talk to me about an unrelated issue. He noticed my bloodshot eyes. He asked that we walk into a conference room to talk. I told him my mother's story. To my amazement, he hugged me tight, and told me about losing his dad and promised to see what he could do to help. A few days later, after I had already forgotten about the conversation, I received a call from him. He was in Washington, DC, on a business trip. He wanted me to email my mother's documents to him. He had visited with someone who knew a senator from Texas. He was going to forward them my mother's medical records and see what they could do.

The next day I received a call from US Senator John Cornyn's office. They promised to see what he could do. His office verified that I indeed had the resources in place to care for my mother. Two days later, the US embassy notified me to send my mother for her visa. The much-awaited phone call came at midnight, US time, which was 8 a.m. in Cameroon, informing me that my mother had been awarded a medical visa by the US embassy. She was especially impressed by the treatment she received this time, and was curious to know who called the embassy on her behalf. That same day, I also received a call from the embassy in Cameroon, and from Senator John Cornyn's office in Washington, confirming that everything was in order for her to travel. They offered further assistance if we needed it. We bought her ticket to travel the very next day.

Everything went incredibly fast after her visa was issued. We were racing against time. My mother arrived late at night, and the next morning her medical team was ready to take care of her. Her CT scans and biopsies confirmed that she indeed had endometrial cancer. They needed to perform the surgery as soon as possible. On day three, she underwent an extensive five-hour procedure. I was with her throughout the ordeal to translate and help calm her fears. She was expected to be in the hospital for four days. On day two, she was doing so well that she was discharged to go home with us. After her wounds healed, she underwent radiation treatment for five weeks. Three months after her operation, she was ready to return home to her husband. At a reception hosted by Dr. Hickle, she got the chance to thank her entire medical team and Senator Cornyn for the incredible care she received, and for truly saving her life.

In the summer of 2012, fourteen Purpose Medical Mission volunteers, including Dr. Hickle, accompanied my mother back to her village. Dr. Hickle also took his thirteen-year-old daughter to introduce her to medical mission work and expose her to the medical field. Last time I checked, she was planning on going to medical school. My pregnant wife, Kyu Mee, and our eleven-month-old son, Zigo, also joined us on this trip. My mother was eager to give my wife a personalized tour of our village. Kyu Mee had waited years to meet my father and the rest of our family living in Cameroon. We had found out she was pregnant after planning this trip. I was a little anxious about her being on antimalarial medications, but she wasn't fazed. She was ready. The children in the village kept Zigo busy while my mother and many sisters kept Kyu Mee entertained. I stayed busy trying to balance my time with my family and our ongoing medical campaign, which turned out to be one of our most successful years for the number of patients seen.

It's been six years at this writing since my mother's cancer diagnosis and treatment, and she is well and healthy. She was able to continue taking care of my father until he died, with her by his side.

Every year after our missions, Father would give us all his usual hugs and would always tell us that we might not see him the next year as he knew that anytime God could call him back. He would give me instructions on how to comfort the family when that happens. He would tell me to make sure everyone knew that he had gone in peace, and had accomplished his work here on earth. He would say this with great certainty. Despite his attempts to prepare us for his passing, I really didn't give it much thought.

And then one day in April 2013, I received a call that he wasn't feeling well and had asked to be taken to the hospital. The initial reports were serious. My mother said he was running a fever and had generalized weakness. I thought probably it was the usual typhoid or malaria, which, with the hospital in Muyuka, was now easily treatable. Reports from his local physician showed that his kidneys were failing. The doctor felt that he would need dialysis, but there were no functioning dialysis centers in the region. I knew that without dialysis, he wasn't going to survive, but I was still hopeful. Within forty-eight hours he had gotten progressively weaker and was occasionally disoriented. I called to speak to him, but all he said to me was to say hello to my family and friends, and then he said "There is time for everything," and handed the phone to my mother.

My mother informed me that he had been very weak and had stopped eating. I spoke to the doctor to get more information on his condition. All he said to me was that "Pa has lost the will to live." He advised me to start making plans to come home. My father passed away on April 12, 2013. He died at Healing Touch Hospital in Muyuka, the hospital that was inspired by his dream for a better, healthier community. He was surrounded by his family, including my mother who consoled me by telling me that she knew that Papa was finally with his mother and the Lord." He was approximately eighty years old. My father left behind many children, biological and adopted, plus thirty-one grandchildren and one great-grandchild. His body was transported to the mortuary at the hospital in Buea to make funeral plans. We made arrangements for all his children, who were now scattered all over the world, to travel to Munyenge to pay their last respects.

Once all the arrangements were made, I would embark on my most emotional journey back to Cameroon to lay my father's body to rest. There were people traveling in from all over the country as well. I didn't know what to expect. When we finally visited the mortuary, I made a striking observation that would help me through the mourning process. In a dim, dark room on the bare floor of the mortuary was my father's body, next to two others. All the bodies were draped from head to toe. However, I could tell which one was my father's, as it was the only body with one leg. When the mortuary assistant undraped his face for us, I noticed that he hadn't lost his smile.

I wasn't sure what his body would look like after a month of being embalmed. He looked so much at peace, almost as if asking us why we were crying. That month after I received the announcement of his death and before traveling for the funeral, I must have cried every day with the thought of my father, and my hero, now gone. But once I was able to see his face, all the tears dried up. He had lived an extraordinary life and now was resting in absolute peace in a place free of pain, suffering, despair or disease. It was all evident on his face.

During the church service, there wasn't enough room for all the guests who had traveled to the village. Neighbors offered their homes to host our guests and hundreds of villagers went out of their way to cook and participate in the funeral. I had never seen anything like it. There were chiefs from his ancestral village and dignitaries from all over the region. During the funeral service, the same priest who had baptized my father over thirty years ago, and presided over my parents' wedding, said Dad's eulogy. He knew my father very well as they worked closely together to make many changes in the village. He reminded us of the day my father accepted God in his life, and how he never looked back after that. He reminded us of his remarkable dedication and commitment to his family, and instructed us to carry on his legacy of being each other's keeper. He told us about my father's stubbornness and distaste for corruption, and of his unorthodox ways of protecting his children, especially his daughters, which earned him many nicknames including *Idi Amin Dada*.

In our tradition, when someone dies outside their ancestral home, they are typically taken back to where they were born. My father had insisted he be buried in Munyenge, the place he had called home for over five decades. It's where all his children were born. More importantly, he wanted to be buried next to his mother, who he had taken from her ancestral home to care for until her until her death with him by her side. She, too, had insisted on being buried in Munyenge where her only three surviving sons lived. Once my father's will was read, we found out that he named me *Fua-keh'bin*, his official successor to carry on the family legacy.

In 2013, upon the request of the administration of Healing Touch Hospital, and approved by the Purpose Medical Mission board of directors, the hospital was renamed John N. Atabong Healing Touch Medical Center, Muyuka, Cameroon, West Africa.

A reception hosted by Dr. Randy Hickle.
My mother's medical team and the other colleagues who assisted in her care.

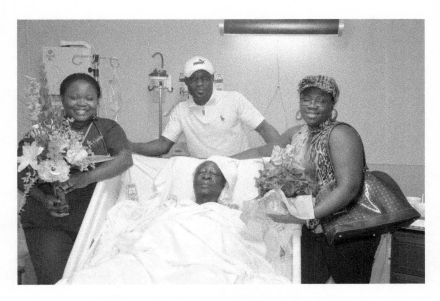

Cameroonian friends visited my mother at the hospital.

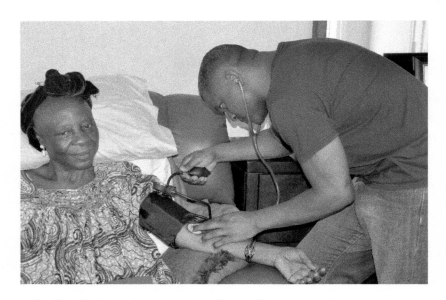

Checking Mom's vital signs at home in Lubbock while she recovers from her operation.

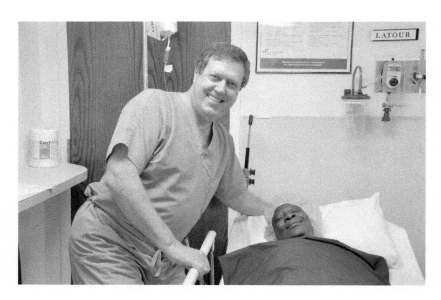

Dr. Duncan Burkholder is one of the doctors who would perform my mother's surgery.

Dr. Randy Hickle meeting my father in Munyenge.

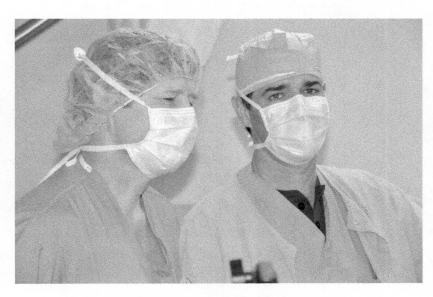

Drs. Randy Hickle (left) and Jonathan Latour (right) during
my mother's procedure at Grace Medical Center in Lubbock.

John N. Atabong Healing Touch Hospital, Muyuka, Cameroon.

John N. Atabong Healing Touch Hospital, Muyuka, Cameroon.

Mother, celebrating her final radiation treatment with her
medical team at Phoenix Oncology.

My father is happy to see his wife return from medical treatment in the US.

My father and Kyu Mee, meeting for the first time.

My mom visits with family members in the United States.

My mother continues to take care of many children at her home in Munyenge.

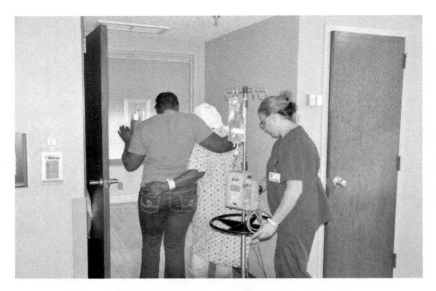

My sister Yvette assists our mother for her first walk after her surgery.

Presenting an appreciation gift from my mother to Senator Cornyn. It's a handmade traditional bag with the inscription, "Greetings From Cameroon."

Mom spending time with her grandchild after her surgery.

With some of my sisters and Mom, visiting Dad's grave site.

EPILOGUE

ABOUT SEVENTY YEARS AFTER my grandmother sent my father away from home to protect his life, my father took that trek out of his ancestral village. Little did he know that this would change the course of history for his future descendants.

My grandmother's decision was made to improve the chance of survival for her three children, after losing nine of them at birth or in the first few years of their lives. Her son, my father, would make several treks for the sake of his children, to provide them with the tools needed for new challenges in an ever-changing world. He sacrificed his life and his health to improve the lives of others around him. He believed in his contribution to perfecting the body of Christ through serving God's creation. He left this world with a smile and a legacy of perseverance and love. He taught me to always fight for good over evil, truth over dishonesty, and peace over despair.

Today, I am the father of two boys, both born 14,000 miles from my ancestral village, in the land of freedom and opportunity. We are in a place where I don't worry about high infant mortality rate. Education comes standard to all. Their challenges will be so different from their ancestors. Like every parent, I too worry about their future. I want to pass on to them a legacy of hard work and sacrifice. I want to give them the tools to fulfill their God-given purpose. If the past seventy years is any indication for the next seventy, then that purpose will be fulfilled by generations of my family to come. The Focolare Movement in Fontem is, vicariously through me, my father's legacy as well.

As we travel the world in search of peace, hope and freedom, we are reminded of the promise God made to the Israelites in Jeremiah 29:11: "For I know the plans I have for you," declares the Lord, "plans to prosper you and not to harm you, plans to give you hope and a future." He doesn't take away our struggles, but instead teaches that through perseverance comes growth. When we struggle through life, we gain the tools we need to withstand obstacles. The harder the fall, the more we remember and gain the experience needed to fight. We are asked to utilize these tools to assist others who may need a little push to get to their destination.

Through all my trips on behalf of Purpose Medical Mission, I have been privileged to meet a president of one country, the vice president of another and many people in positions of extreme power. Some days I ask myself: why else would a kid from a little village in Africa be able to have such honor to see, laugh with, pray with, and even make friends with these individuals from all over the world? Because I am called to be the voice of the voiceless. Because we are given power and access to represent the powerless. Because we are a bridge to deliver the most basic health needs that I believe everyone in the world deserves access to.

The most fulfilling experience has been meeting the people in some of these remote villages that we serve. I see me in them and hope that they see themselves in me. I pray that my story inspires them and their children, to see that they, too, are created perfectly in God's image for a purpose only they can accomplish. I pray that they see that through the obstacles in life, they too can gather the knowledge to withstand their challenges of tomorrow, and to let Christ's light and glory shine through their struggles and their sufferings. In the end, they, too, can make their own small contributions in their communities to leave their world a better place than they found it.

I was once asked by a journalist who had accompanied us for the opening of one of our clinics, "What's next, Sixtus?" My answer then and now is that we will go wherever we are called to serve.

Meeting with Dr. Ben Carson, renowned neurosurgeon and
Secretary of the US Department of Housing and Urban Development.

Meeting with President Enrique Bolanos of Nicaragua.

Meeting with US Senator John Cornyn of Texas and Texas governor, Greg Abbott.

With my sisters Hannah and Clementine.

With US Congressman
Jodey Arrington of Texas.

With Vice President Rafael
Espada of Guatemala.

Acknowledgments

Thanks to my publisher, Koehler Books, for taking a chance on me, and to my editors, Joe Coccaro and Elizabeth Marshall McClure, for bringing my story to life.

Thanks to the Purpose Medical Mission Board of Directors for making my dream a reality, and to our many volunteers and sponsors for being an extension of God's healing hands.

Last but not least, thank you Dr. Richard George, MD, for being my mentor and trusted advisor.

I'd also like to thank Carmen Ng, Stephanie Schmidt, Alicia Morris Groos, William Davis II, Josephine Ncho, and the law office of Norton Rose Fulbright.

In Loving Memory of

Pa John N. Atabong

CPSIA information can be obtained
at www.ICGtesting.com
Printed in the USA
BVHW03s0726170818
524506BV00024B/11/P